Majestic
and
Wild

MAJESTIC
AND
WILD

TRUE STORIES *of* FAITH *and*
ADVENTURE *in the* GREAT OUTDOORS

MURRAY PURA

BakerBooks

a division of Baker Publishing Group
Grand Rapids, Michigan

© 2013 by Murray Pura

Published by Baker Books
a division of Baker Publishing Group
P.O. Box 6287, Grand Rapids, MI 49516-6287
www.bakerbooks.com

Printed in the United States of America

Library of Congress Cataloging-in-Publication Data
Pura, Murray, 1954-
    Majestic and wild : true stories of faith and adventure in the great outdoors / Murray Pura.
        p. cm.
    Summary: "Avid outdoorsman tells exciting stories of his wilderness adventures that reveal spiritual lessons not easily learned in church or in our everyday lives"—Provided by publisher.
    ISBN 978-0-8010-1512-0 (pbk. : alk. paper)
    1. Nature—Religious aspects—Christianity. I. Title.
BT695.5.P87 2013
242—dc23   2012035839

All these stories are true, but in some instances names, locations, and circumstances have been altered in order to ensure privacy and preserve anonymity.

The internet addresses, email addresses, and phone numbers in this book are accurate at the time of publication. They are provided as a resource. Baker Publishing Group does not endorse them or vouch for their content or permanence.

Author is represented by Les Stobbe, Literary Agent.

13   14   15   16   17   18   19   7   6   5   4   3   2   1

For Yukon 1986–2001 & Nahanni 1986–2002

We never grew tired of the thousands of trails.
We never grew tired of each other.
We never grew tired of God and what he had made.
We were always glad of a life together
and a wilderness shared.

Contents

Contents

Lord, our Lord, how majestic is your name in all
the earth!

Psalm 8:9

Trailhead

Men to Match My Mountains

> For, lo, he that formeth the mountains, and crea-
> teth the wind, and declareth unto man what is his
> thought, that maketh the morning darkness, and
> treadeth upon the high places of the earth, The
> Lord, The God of hosts, is his name.
>
> Amos 4:13 KJV

On July 4, 1894, Sam Walter Foss wrote, "Bring me men to match my mountains . . . bring me men to match my forests."[1]
John Muir penned,

> Climb the mountains and get their good tidings. Nature's
> peace will flow into you as sunshine flows into trees. The
> winds will blow their own freshness into you, and the storms
> their energy, while cares will drop off like the autumn leaves.[2]

1. Sam Walter Foss, "The Coming American," 1894.
2. John Muir, *Our National Parks* (New York: Houghton, Mifflin and Company, 1901), 56.

13

It had been a hard climb that took several hours.

But I didn't feel like a conqueror of mountains or a man brimming over with energy and peace at the moment. I needed a few minutes' rest and a mouthful of cold water.

My favorite hunting rifle, a Remington Sendero built in 1992 or 1993, was strapped tightly to my back. When Boss Clay—Mister Isaac Henry Clayton—said it was time for a break and a swallow of water, I squatted among the rocks and scrub pine, took the firearm in my hands, and examined it for nicks or scratches before I did anything else, much as I wanted to pop the top off my canteen. The rifle had a stainless steel barrel and fittings set in a black fiberglass stock with a thin spidery pattern. An engraved plate by the trigger guard said the Sendero was a gift for Pale Rider from his friends at the North Island Rod and Gun Club in British Columbia, Canada. My nickname was a play on the western by the same name in which Clint Eastwood portrays an avenging angel who stalks the bad guys in the guise of an ordained minister. My profession of ordained minister at least partially fit.

A 7 mm Remington Magnum, the rifle could take down any game on the North American continent. I have never been of the opinion I needed a howitzer or an air strike by the USS *Abraham Lincoln* to bring down grizzly or moose or even a Kodiak. As a hunting rifle, the Sendero fitted the bill and was more than enough.

I looked up at the ridge where we were heading. A few more steps and we would be at the tree line. Beyond that, we would be making our way over bare rock and scree and easily noticeable to our prey unless we moved very slowly. I glanced through my 3x9 Bausch and Lomb scope. It was elk we were after, and they were trailing each other up a rocky path that wound around the shoulder of the mountain. We needed to take a shot within the next ten minutes.

Boss Clay, father of one of my friends, had crawled up to the last few trees and was using his binoculars. "At the bend they'll have to slow down to let the ones ahead of them negotiate the turn. There will be a nice flank shot. You should be able to get your first elk."

I crouched beside him, Pale Rider still in my hands. "Which one should I scope?"

"See that elk about tenth in line? He's an eight point. Beautiful bull. That's the one. Don't move out from the trees if you can help it. It's four hundred yards. Use your bipod."

I unfolded the stainless steel bipod from under the Sendero's stock. Going prone, I settled the stock firmly into my shoulder and sighted in on the bull, choosing a spot just behind his massive left shoulder. I played with the set of the bipod on the rocky ground until there was no more wobble. Another minute and the bull was slowing as the ones just ahead stopped while several others picked their way around the curve in the trail and disappeared.

"Okay," said Boss quietly. "Get your breathing down. Remember to squeeze, not pull, and you'll have meat for your family right through the winter."

I got my breathing under control, kept the scope tightly on the bull as it came to a standstill for a few moments, slipped the safety off the Sendero, chambered a round, and counted to ten in my head. My finger rested on the trigger and slowly began to move in toward my body. Seven . . . eight . . . nine . . .

"Stop. Don't shoot."

I froze. "What?"

"Ease up."

"But I've got him right where I want him—"

"Ease up."

I took my finger off the trigger and brought my eye away from the scope. Boss pointed. I lifted my head and saw a knot of elk forming at the curve, bringing all forward movement to a dead stop. Cows and calves milled around in confusion and then began to head back along the ridge the way they'd come. This made my bull even more of a target as elk trotted past him, isolating him momentarily against a skyline of silver clouds.

"I could take him, Boss," I protested.

"Maybe. But I doubt you'd ever harvest the meat."

"Why not? It'll only take fifteen minutes to get to him."

"Something's spooking the herd. My bet is it's not hunters crawling around on the other side of the mountain."

Elk that had already rounded the bend were reappearing, obviously distraught, swinging their heads and pushing those in front of them to move faster. There were grunts and snorts and cries. My bull elk finally bellowed and turned around, stepping quickly and surely along the mountain track. My perfect shot was gone. I still did not understand why Boss had ordered me not to fire.

As we watched the cows and bulls head along the ridge, scatter across the rocky slope, and make for the forest half a mile to our right, a burly shape emerged on the trail they had abandoned at the shoulder of the mountain. The creature stopped, lifted a shaggy head, and took in scent. Satisfied, it continued to pursue the elk with a steady, unconcerned, shambling gait. A silvertip grizzly.

Boss grunted. "I figured. Let me tell you something that happened to friends of mine when they were hunting elk in the Rockies."

Boss continued, "The married couple were footing it up-slope over rugged terrain like us. A bull moved into the open from a cluster of pine trees and stood perfectly still, sampling the air. The husband had a clear three hundred yard shot and took it. The bull jumped and crashed to the ground. Keeping their eyes on the spot as well as they could, the man and woman moved in on the kill.

"But something else was moving in on the kill at the same time. A male grizzly, alerted by the shot, had begun to head in the general direction of the sound. The bear had learned that such a sound often meant a dead animal it would be able to feed on. As it half ran toward the region of the gunshot, its nose picked up the scent of blood and the bear altered direction slightly. Within five minutes it had located the dead or dying bull. One swat made sure it wasn't going anywhere. The grizzly began to eat.

"It took the couple closer to twenty-five minutes to find the elk. No sooner did they see the bull's head and antlers than the grizzly raised itself up from its feeding, spotted them, and flew into an immediate rage—this was its kill and it meant to protect it from marauders. Before the couple had a chance to raise their rifles, the bear ripped into them, claws and fangs slashing. They were torn and battered within minutes. They rolled as far from the kill site as they could—the grizzly literally breathing and biting down on their necks—before stopping and feigning death. The bear continued to swat and nip, then went back to the kill. Long after the grizzly had left them alone and returned to the elk carcass, the pair helped each other crawl slowly down the slope to their vehicle. Both survived.

"Now, what would have happened here?" Boss continued, his eyes following the silvertip as it rumbled toward the forest where the elk had fled. "You'd have dropped your bull. We would have started up the slope to harvest the kill and that would have taken maybe ten or fifteen minutes. The grizzly comes around the corner while we're still making our way, spots the body, and claims it for its own. Where do we hide from a grizzly on that barren mountainside? It scents us, finally gets a look at us, and decides we're entirely too close to its food source for its liking. It charges. Maybe we survive the attack, maybe we don't. If we do, we're torn up pretty bad. You lose an eye, say, and I lose an arm. Or one of us bleeds out. Say it's you. I have to tell that young wife of yours with a baby on the way that her husband's dead. No thanks. I expect you were ready to thank God for a winter's supply of elk steaks and roasts. Well, now you can try the flip side of the coin. Thank God for the perfect shot you never took and the perfect kill you never made."

It was a long, cold hike back through the trees to the dirt road and the truck. Small white flakes began to spin swiftly out of the gray sky. In the cab, our thermoses still held warm coffee and we gulped it down. Boss turned the keys in the ignition and the truck growled loudly. Suddenly he twisted the keys again and turned the engine off. He looked at me.

"What?" I asked, impatient to get going.

"Just a second. There's something we neglected to do."

Under my boots was about three feet of hamburger wrappers, french fry cartons, .308 cartridges, Tim Hortons paper coffee cups, Cabela's and Bass Pro fall hunting catalogs, and a jar of dried up peanut butter. Boss rooted around, asking me to lift my feet, then grumbled and reached across to open the glove compartment. Out spilled more cartridges, two very stiff and very old hot dogs, a bundle of forestry maps to locate hunting districts, and a Bible bound in buckskin. It was the Bible he wanted.

He flipped the pages until he found the spot. Then he put a hand inside his jacket, plucked a pair of glasses from a pocket, planted them on his nose, and read out loud one of the most familiar verses in the Bible: "And we know that all things work together for good to them that love God, to them who are the called according to his purpose" (Romans 8:28

KJV). Glancing over the top of his glasses at me, he asked, "Okay?"

"God wanted me not to harvest the bull elk."

Boss made a face. "God wanted you not to get killed. God wanted you to learn a lesson about bears and hunting skills. God wanted you to take the lesson home with you and apply it the next time you are out in the field—or behind the pulpit at church."

"How's that?"

Boss closed the Bible, laid it aside, and started the engine a second time. A mixture of warm and cool air blew on us from the heater. He put the truck into gear. The snowflakes were larger and falling more thickly.

"You wanted to harvest a bull. God had something else in mind for you to get your head around—not you killing an elk, but avoiding a grizzly killing you on another hunting trip. It's like this: suppose you go into church and preach this great sermon, but no one gets it. No one is grateful. They think it's a wash. So you're crushed. The Sunday's a loss as far as you and your ministry are concerned. You tell your wife to go ahead—you'll walk home because you need to have some time alone. The church is empty; everyone has gone home. You go to your study and shut the door. You pray. You feel pretty bad.

"Then this guy shows up who missed the whole service, but finds you in your office. He was passing through town and hoped a church would be open and a pastor available. He needs counseling, needs prayer. He was on his way to kill himself but decided to stop and talk to a man of God. You call your wife and explain you'll be late and spend the afternoon with him. He gives his life to Christ and the urge to commit suicide vanishes.

"The guy sticks around for the evening service and tells everyone what happened to him. A year later you hear from him and he's attending a school in Dallas and training for the ministry. Wow. All because you thought you didn't score with the sermon so you stayed behind to pray, something you wouldn't have done if you had nailed your sermon and gone home happy with your wife. You thought you'd missed out. But a life was saved because things didn't go as you planned. Same thing with the bull elk up on the ridge and the silvertip around the corner. You thought you'd missed out. But what you missed out on actually saved our lives. You see?"

My head was whirling with Boss's words, but tied into Romans 8:28 they made perfect sense. "I do."

Boss nodded and the truck lurched forward along the logging road. "There's always takeaway from the mountains and the wilderness. Always. Not just food on the table or a great photograph or a really beautiful sunset—I mean spiritual takeaway—a word from God. Something different, something you don't get from the cities and towns and freeways. Do you understand what I mean?"

A whitetail bounded across our track. Boss hit the brakes as I put my hand to the dashboard to brace myself. I watched the doe disappear among the dark green trees. They were already thick with snow that was as white as the blaze of tail that shot up from the deer as it ran.

"I do understand, Boss," I said. "God and the wilderness are tied together in ways nothing else on earth is. It's not man-made. And it stays unique so long as man doesn't corrupt it."

He nodded and smiled as the truck surged forward again. "Yeah. That's it. Absolutely."

1

The Split Hoof Killer

Do not be afraid of the terrors of the night, nor
the arrow that flies in the day. Do not dread the
disease that stalks in darkness, nor the disaster
that strikes at midday.

Psalm 91:5–6 NLT

When people ask me how it happened and what it was like I
say, "Have you ever felt you had to run for your life and then
realized as you ran that there was no way on earth you were
going to make it?"

The day was a glorious one—blue skies and sunshine and
summer trees thick with green. Our young family piled into
our Jeep Cherokee and drove through miles of forests and
foothills, the Rocky Mountains at our backs. We spotted
deer and coyote and sometimes, way up a hillside, a black
bear or young grizzly. Eventually, we stopped at a picnic site
and sat down at an outdoor table to eat lunch. The kids
were only three or four at the time and were soon laughing

21

on the swings, bouncing on the teeter-totter, and zipping down the slides.

I played with them a while, then asked if anyone wanted to walk the dogs with me. My son and daughter, Micah and Micaela, liked to go on short hikes, but the playground in the woods was a novelty so they wanted to stay behind. This meant that my young wife, Linda, was staying behind as well to keep an eye on them. She gave me a kiss and bent down to pet Yukon and Nahanni.

"Enjoy yourself, Mur. I wish I could come with you. It's a perfect day."

I put the dogs on their six-foot leashes. We soon found a narrow path that led away from the picnic area and began to follow it. Yukon and Nahanni were a Golden Labrador and coyote cross—they had big Lab eyes, Lab loyalty and intelligence, but their muzzles were coyote long, their ears up and coyote sharp, and their tails coyote thick and bushy, with white tips. Often they moved so silently in the yard or, when invited, in the house that I didn't even know they were standing behind me. Yukon was the brother, Nahanni the sister.

After about ten minutes among the trees we came out into the open and made our way through a large patch of grassland. Glimpses of the mountains in the distance and that shimmering sea of blue over my head made me literally thank God I was alive—his creation, as always, filled me with wonder, exhilaration, and peace. The companionship of Yukon and Nahanni made the experience that much sweeter. Our trail took us farther and farther from the woods behind us and bent toward a new stretch of forest a hundred yards ahead.

A sudden crashing of branches snapped me out of my thoughts and prayers and brought the dogs' heads up sharply. A huge brown creature hurtled out of the woods at us, its large ears flat, its eyes rolled back white, its teeth flashing.

At first I thought it was a wild horse. But the size and long legs and hump on its back told me something else—moose. I had seen moose in the wild before, but never before had one been charging at me and bawling out its fury.

I did not react instantly. For the longest time—two or three seconds—I watched the moose come barreling down the trail and could not believe what was happening. Then I unsnapped the leashes and the dogs took off the way we had come at top speed, as fast as greyhounds, as swift as timber wolves. I turned and raced through the tall grass for a thin strip of trees on my left. Glancing behind, I saw that the moose had quickly decided it could not catch the dogs. It was roaring across the grass to cut me off.

I shouted out loud, "Lord!" That was the only prayer I could utter. Then I tried to run faster than I had ever run before. I knew that moose could reach speeds of up to thirty-five miles per hour. Without God's help, I was not going to make it.

I was into the trees only seconds before the moose. I would no sooner get behind one tree trunk than it would crane its neck and chop with its teeth and I would dart behind another. Then it would come at me again, its eyes wild, blowing loudly from its nostrils, always trying to snag my head or arm in its mouth and bite down as it bent its neck around the tree. For several minutes I sprang behind tree after tree, my hands bracing against each trunk, staring right into the moose's white and black eyes. It was only inches from my face.

Farther and farther I went into the forest and farther and farther it charged in after me, lunging with its head and teeth, striking out with its front hooves, tearing great strips of bark off the trees, shaking its great shaggy head from side to side and bellowing its rage. I could smell the stench of its breath and the reek of its fur.

Suddenly I saw it glance back over its shoulder. It was worried about something—what? Then a thought came to me: *There must be a calf. This is the mother and she is afraid the dogs are going to attack her baby while she is chasing me through the woods.*

The moose made its decision. It blasted hot breath into my face with a final howl that made it seem half animal and half demon. But it broke off the assault. Crashing back through the trees to the open grassland, it lumbered toward the brush where it had first exploded onto the trail. I watched it go, not daring to move from behind the sheltering poplars. There were only a few dozen of them, with slender trunks that nevertheless had been thick enough to save my life. As I waited and tracked the moose's movements, a white shape came carefully through the trees toward me—Yukon! My male dog had not deserted me but, despite great danger to himself, had lingered nearby and was coming now to make sure I was all right. I found out later that Nahanni ran all the way back to the picnic area and dropped at the children's feet, panting. My wife wondered, somewhat annoyed, how I could be so irresponsible and careless as to leave my dogs off leash and unattended in a wilderness area.

Yukon and I began to make our way out of the strip of trees I had plunged into. The cow moose stood a little ways down the trail, its head bent back and its eyes glaring death at us as we emerged from the woods. She seemed ready to attack again at any moment, and I was in no hurry to get too far from the shelter of the poplars. I moved slowly. The moose watched for any hint that we were altering direction toward her calf. I walked and stopped, walked and stopped, Yukon staying close. Each step away from her was a step won and she granted us our steady retreat. Finally we reached a point where she didn't care about us anymore and stalked into the trees where her calf was hidden.

I took a moment to examine the damp mud on the path, something I had not done when the dogs and I had first begun our walk—after all, it had not been a hunting trip. There were my size 13 EE boot marks. There were the paw prints of my Lab-coyote dogs. There were the large sharp points of a mature moose's tracks—and there were the small sharp points of a very tiny moose's hoofprints, a moose that was the miniature of a mother that outweighed it by as much as 700 pounds.

Days later I would read about the frequency and lethality of cow moose attacks in North America. A friend from church in the Royal Canadian Mounted Police (RCMP) warned me they were a constant threat to people who worked in the bush and had killed loggers, surveyors, park wardens, and tree planters. "I'd sooner take my chances with a mother grizzly robbed of its cubs," he said, "than take on a cow moose protecting its calf. It will come after you with its teeth or its front hooves. And it won't stop until you're dead."

I could never have outrun the moose let alone survive its assault. The small strip of trees to my left were all that stood between me and its killing rage. I might just as easily have followed the dogs in their wild flight down the trail. Why didn't I do that? What made me choose the small patch of woods to my left and risk the hazardous sprint to reach them? Something built into me had known a run down the trail would not succeed while a race into the trees might. Instinct said to flee—but flee where? That God-made part within sized up the situation and sent my body hurtling over the field. It reminded me of the psalm writer's words from Psalm 139 verses 13 and 14: "For you created my inmost being; you knit me together in my mother's womb. I praise you because I am fearfully and wonderfully made."

God's creation is amazing. But there are two faces to it. One moment I'm basking in the sunshine and admiring God's mountains and woods and sky, and the next I'm running for my life from a creature that is part of that godly creation. Why? Because while creation can be unbelievably beautiful, the flip side is that it can be unbelievably dangerous. We live in a fallen world. Eden is long gone, and sin has marred the perfection that once existed. Only in the new heaven and new earth has God promised to remove the hazards and allow the wolf to lie down with the lamb and a child to play happily with a snake.

Paul explained this dynamic in Romans 8:20–21: "Against its will all creation was subjected to God's curse. But with eager hope, the creation looks forward to the day when it will join God's children in glorious freedom from death and decay" (NLT).

The cow moose attack was a terrifying experience. But it was also an experience that brought me a deeper understanding of how I am made, how creation is made, and how—despite the dangers and the brokenness—God still works in that creation and through that creation to bring about his perfect will. It was also an experience that brought about praise and thanks right from my heart—I was so glad to be alive and be a survivor.

Regardless of the risks involved, God's world remains an incredible place to be and offers a stunning and rugged wilderness for people to discover and explore, a place that can take us into the presence of the Master of heaven and earth, who dreamed the whole thing up and put it all together.

2

Black Bart

And he was with the wild animals, and the angels were ministering to him.

Mark 1:13 ESV

Whenever I think of Jesus being with animals it brings to mind those animals present at his birth, at his Crucifixion (where Roman officers would have been mounted on horses), on Palm Sunday (when he rode into Jerusalem on a donkey), and during his forty days in the desert wilderness amongst the foxes, jackals, wolves, and lions. I like to think there was an understanding between those wild animals and him. There's no mention of them being aggressive. I get the impression they were wandering about in the same places as Jesus, sharing the same watering hole, sometimes close by, other times distant. After a couple of weeks, I suspect they remained wary but more accepting of his presence in their world. Or perhaps not so wary. He was human, yes, but he was also the God who made them. They may have sensed a unique relationship that allowed them to bond to him.

I've had that experience of unusual closeness with wild animals. Mule deer and whitetails and elk have let me get close. Coyotes too. Wolves and foxes not so much. But, now and then, a bear and I have been eye-to-eye and both of us have lived to talk about it.

It was a Sunday morning a few hours before church. Yukon and Nahanni and I were on one of our many back roads, not so far from houses and streets as to consider ourselves deep in the wilderness, not so close that we had to worry about cars and trucks or people out for an early stroll. The dogs were both off leash—I trusted them enough at that point to know their training had taken hold and they would not bolt after deer or other animals. My mind was elsewhere: on the morning service, the message I'd be preaching, what I'd be doing after church. The dogs had trotted around a bend in the trail and were out of sight. Hands in my jeans pockets, I kicked a stone. A loud bark snapped my head up.

My dogs were not barkers. When they did it, I knew the difference between play barks, barks of anger, and the kind they used just to get attention. This was a deep and loud bark I'd never heard before, and I was pretty sure it was from Yukon, the male. I hurried around the curve.

The black bear was big and was hardly six feet from me. I froze. Yukon and Nahanni stood between us, bodies taut as bowstrings. The bear scarcely gave me a glance. He was on all fours staring at the dogs. There was no growling, no snapping of the jaws, no hostility in his eyes. He waited to see what the dogs were going to do; the dogs waited to see what he was going to do.

Before I could think of what commands to give or how to act to defuse the situation, the bear took off, racing up the trail in a flurry of dust. About a hundred feet from us he stopped dead, wheeled around, and stared back at Yukon and Nahanni and me. I got the strongest impression he had never seen dogs or humans before. Perhaps this was the first time he had ventured out of the deep rain forest, a place lacking evidence of human activity or presence. He was still looking back when I turned the dogs around and headed off in a completely different direction to finish our walk.

I had never been that close to a bear before, so for that reason alone I never forgot the incident. I certainly did not expect to see the bear again. But a few weeks later, I was standing on our front lawn on a September evening and saw movement in the bushes near our neighbor's apple tree. A black bear emerged, got on his hind legs, and began to shake the branches so that apples plopped onto the grass. He then began to stuff them into his mouth. I took a step forward and he spun his head around to look at me. Then he got up and shook the branches again.

When six or seven more apples had fallen he dropped back onto all fours and began to crunch them up between his jaws. After every second apple he lifted his head to glance in my direction. Then he'd return to the serious business of eating. Once he had finished his meal he stood still for a few minutes and gazed at me. I knew who he was. There was a ragged notch cut out of his left ear that I remembered from that moment on the trail when we were no more than a few feet apart. He decided to amble away, taking one last apple in his teeth.

Black Bart, I decided to name him. Black Bart the Apple Thief. I wondered if he had been gazing at me because he also recalled our encounter in the bush and was wondering where those furry four-footed companions of mine were.

Dogs and bear saw each other again a day later. I had walked my dogs off our property, across a small highway, and up into the hills and forest. Along a logging road the dogs stopped and stared—a large bear came out of the woods and began to lumber down the road toward us. He shrugged aside a fallen tree in his path and kept coming, never lifting his head. Not recognizing the bear, I got the dogs turned around quickly and we headed to the bottom of the road. Once the bear reached the place where we had been, he stopped as if he'd hit a wall. Then he dove into the bushes. A moment later, his head popped up, revealing the familiar gaze of his eyes and the notch in the ear.

It was Black Bart all right. The dogs began to whine and move their tails—did they recognize him too? Did they know his particular scent, or were they just excited because it was a bear, any old bear? Black Bart and the dogs looked at each other with about fifty yards between them. Finally Bart slipped his head back among the leaves and disappeared.

For a few weeks that fall Bart showed up everywhere—in huckleberry patches, climbing trees, moving slowly through undergrowth. We never got too close, but there was always his stare, his popping in and out of a hiding place, running away, but always wanting to look back. And then came the days he stopped running and just gazed at the three of us, unafraid, unconcerned, pausing at whatever he was doing, going back to it when it suited him. Throughout October we grew to expect to see him as much as we expected to see trees and rocks and birds. He became a fixture in the forest we hiked in. The sight of the bear and his lack of fear was a welcome diversion for whatever weighed on my mind on any given day.

Who else he saw, what he did when he spotted them, whether he stopped running from all dogs and humans, I never knew. We didn't see anyone else when we walked. There were only the wild creatures of the woods and, every two or three days, an encounter with Black Bart. So maybe that's what it was like for Jesus when he walked about in the desert among the animals he had created. Maybe it felt completely natural for him to be there with them—like it had been completely natural for Adam and Eve in the garden that was Eden.

One day I was in the rain forest alone with a rifle in my hands. I could take a doe and I had a tag for a bear. I actually had not seen Bart for over a week and was not thinking about him. I was just concentrating on stepping slowly and carefully through the forest and along the paths that I knew so well. A mist came down and settled like silver dust over the ferns and cedars. I left the woods and began to move along one of the many old logging roads the dogs and I hiked. There was a dark shape in the tall grass at the edge of the track—a bear. I lifted my rifle and looked quickly through my scope. The notch on the left ear was unmistakable. So was the fixed gaze.

I did not anthropomorphize Bart other than giving him his name. He ate berries and carrion and fish, he lived in a den without a pillow for his head or a blanket to cover his body, he did not speak English or French or Spanish, and he did not read books or the Bible before he went to sleep. He was a bear, not a human. But I lowered my firearm and gazed back at him as I had done so many times before. There was no way I was going to shoot him.

His stare was different, as if he could smell the steel and grease of my gun and did not care for the scent. It seemed as if he was watching me more carefully than he ever had since we first met on that other logging road a Sunday morning months before. You can call it crazy, but I believe he sensed I could do him harm and was waiting to see what I would do with the bad smelling stick I held in my hands. He may have picked up on my adrenaline too—who knows? But his look was intense, not easy and relaxed like it had been for the past few weeks whenever he recognized that it was the dogs and me that he had encountered yet again.

He waited and I waited. I did not lift the rifle a second time. Finally, apparently satisfied that he could safely turn his back on me, he ambled forward and melted into the mist and the forest. Days later I was walking with the dogs along the same road and his prints were still in the dirt. But now, looking for Bart, we could not find him. Weeks went by. We never saw the bear again.

Bart might have been shot, though I never heard that anyone got a black bear in that particular region. It's more likely he moved farther back into the forests for the winter, farther back and higher up into the hills and mountains. The following spring, he might have decided to explore west toward the open sea or just stay in the interior, well away from all roads and 4x4s and chance encounters with humans. I only know this is something many hunters and wilderness campers and backpackers have experienced—wild creatures that are neither friend nor foe, but companions with us, if only for a few minutes or hours in our journeys through the wilderness and the hidden places of both the earth and our lives. Perhaps this is what Jesus experienced—animals offering a quiet friendship or tolerance that removes, for a time, the burden of human loneliness.

3

Cougar at the Door

The lions roar for their prey and seek their food
from God.

Psalm 104:21

Most of us have seen cougars on television nature shows or
in movies, zoos, or wilderness parks. Beautiful creatures, they
are nevertheless powerful and lethal predators and have killed
their share of deer and, sometimes, humans. So having one
with an attitude show up in your backyard is not something
you wish for.

A rainbow trout stream runs through our property, and that
stream has its source in a box canyon in the Rocky Mountains.
Paths run along its banks where the creek passes through
town. Deer move along the paths, back and forth, across the
fast-flowing waters. Sometimes cougar follow them, padding
down out of the mountains and foothills.

It's not as if I didn't know cougar could take the path to our door. My son and daughter had been locked down at their school for several hours when they were young because a cougar had been spotted on the school grounds. It stalked and killed a whitetail and decided to stay in the vicinity until it had consumed the carcass. Eventually it was darted, caged, and transported out of the region.

And it wasn't as if I didn't know how dangerous they were. A cougar will choose to hunt humans without provocation, whereas with a grizzly, you have to get between a sow and its cubs to get into real trouble. Or stray near a grizzly's kill, startle it, or have the misfortune to run up against one that is wounded or rogue. The cougar that is hunting comes looking for trouble, taking pets, livestock, sometimes children, and even adults.

I've listened to park staff who are trained to downplay the threat of cougars. I respect that they don't want people up in arms calling for open season on the big cats. This has happened at times to the wolf, with tragic consequences for their wilderness existence. However, I have seen parents walk their children to school bus stops with large iron bars in their hands to fend off cougar attacks. I have lived in places where the cats have taken boys and girls in their jaws and run off.

Still, I was surprised when my son Micah and I pulled into our driveway one Saturday morning in the spring and our neighbors immediately met us to share about a cougar that had padded out of the trees in the nearby campground and strode over their front lawn and ours. I had that sense of unbelief you get when you haven't personally witnessed some dramatic event happen, but instead live it vicariously through someone else's story.

"Haven't they caught it yet?" I asked my neighbors, startled.

"No," they told me.

"Well then, where is it? Where did it go?"

"No one knows. It could have headed back into the hills or it could still be around here somewhere."

I lit out for the back of our house and the dog run.

Cougars don't like dogs and neither do bears. Dogs infuriate bears and frighten cougars—unless the dogs don't bark. Then the cougars eat them. That's how other neighbors across the street had lost their Alaskan Malamute. I didn't want to lose my canine companions the same way.

I thanked God that they were still in their run and that the cougar hadn't sprung in and attacked them. I quickly got our dogs into the garage and locked the door after making sure they had plenty of water. Micah had gone into the house, telling his mother and sister to stay indoors. Then the two of us went back to the front.

Now seemingly everybody was out there. The RCMP, Fish and Wildlife, bylaw officers—and the cougar dogs. Straining at their leashes, they whined and barked and definitely had got hold of a scent from the campground. A dozen armed men moved off into the trees and bushes that lined the campsites and creek bank.

My son and I went to the backyard and walked along the path that followed the trout stream. We watched the cougar dogs and their handlers and the other officers head upstream into town. For the longest time nothing happened. Then they were hustling back along the path on the other side of the creek and fanning out through the tall green cottonwood trees opposite our house. We strained our eyes. Was something flitting through the shadows and high grass and tree trunks? Moving with the smooth flow of water and air and light?

The cougar, or mountain lion, is a beautiful creature. At first glance the head seems too small for the body and the tail impossibly long. But when you take another look you realize the big cat has been wonderfully and intelligently put together by the hand of God and the forces of creation he set in motion. This North American lion, like its African counterpart, is a work of art—lethal and to be treated with utmost caution and respect. A well-executed combination of muscle, bone, speed, and strength that leaps with freedom and grace.

Frightening as a cougar on the prowl can be, here was one bringing the spirit of freedom and God and the wilderness with him as he ran from the men, guns, and dogs. He holed up in an old culvert in the hillside, all two hundred pounds of him. A big cat hiding away in a narrow pipe to escape those who meant him harm. But not too much harm.

People who live near the wild places often remember eventually that something in them wants to care for creation, nurture it, and not blight or destroy the wildness of those beasts who move freely within such a harsh and beautiful world.

A large trap was placed in front of the culvert, flash bangs were set off at the other end of the pipe, and the cat scrambled out into the cage in a panic. A couple of days later, still lean and fierce, it was released back into its domain of crags, caves, and wind-blasted pine to hunt and sleep and roar. But behind it the cat left with me another measure of holy strength in my heart and in the heart of my son.

I never stop marveling when I see God's creatures in their natural setting of trees and peaks and wild waters. What a breath of fresh air they are to the soul. Our streets are crammed with cars and trucks, our houses stuffed together on narrow streets, our air filled with dust and exhaust, our ears with screeching tires and rumbling engines. But where they live there is liberty—the distances are vast and uncluttered, the air clean and unfettered, the only sounds wind and water and hawk cries or the great forest's hush, which is a silence with a sound all its own.

Dangerous many of these places and its creatures are, but also exhilarating—who would want to be in a world without them? This would be a world always leashed and restrained, always predictable and under our control, always safe and sound. Just being in the woods and mountains has saved my sanity and brought me clarity, peace, and a walk with God nothing else could provide. How often I have thanked him for his creation and the wild spirit still alive in it, hazardous as that environment can be. It is such a place of heart, such a place for those who long to be utterly free in the Lord. "Light, space, zest—that's God!" (Psalm 27:1 THE MESSAGE).

4

The Grizzly I Couldn't Shoot

All the days ordained for me were written in your book before one of them came to be.

Psalm 139:16

It was meant to be a deer hunt.

There were a few rules. Between the power lines and the highway—no deer stands, no feeding stations, no does, shotgun only, 00 buckshot.

I knew the area well from running my dogs. Lots of brush and trees, saskatoons and huckleberries growing in large patches, old logging roads, boulders and rocks, and not much in the way of open country.

The shotgun I picked out was nothing special, but it was sturdy—a single shot twelve gauge built like a tank, with a twenty-eight-inch barrel. The full choke would keep the pattern of the nine pellets tight. I put it in the back of my jeep with a box of shotgun shells, threw on my olive drab fly-fishing vest with all its pockets, and headed for the hills.

The weather was a toss-up—some clouds, some sun, a hint of rain, no wind. I parked to the side of a logging road well below the power lines and their towers. Put some two-and-three-quarter-inch shells in one of my vest pockets with a bag of trail mix. Loaded the shotgun. And set out.

I moved slowly and silently along overgrown roadways and paths. I never saw anyone else. I crept a half mile one way, crept a half mile back another way, and never saw any deer. Then I decided to hide myself behind a boulder at a spot in the bush where several deer trails converged. There were fresh tracks, so I was hopeful.

Hunting whitetail with a shotgun is a very different challenge from hunting them with a rifle and a scope or crouching all morning in a stand—you have to get in very close. Even a traditional black powder rifle will give you more range than a shotgun with 00 buck. The chances of getting within thirty to fifty yards of a stag without him picking up your scent or movement are slim, but it can be done. Sometimes you are just plain lucky to surprise one. Or blessed.

After an hour and a half cramped up behind the boulder I decided to try for higher ground. I was basically in a kind of foothills environment, with white-capped mountains to the west. I knew there were several rocky outcrops in the hunting zone that might offer some success with a buck. I began to move along the trails again, stepping slowly and quietly, until I reached the first knoll. I scanned it carefully and began to climb, stopping every few moments to look and listen. But I saw nothing in the way of deer. So I ate some trail mix, climbed down, walked a couple of hundred yards, and tried another knoll. Nothing.

On the third, a whitetail lifted its large tail and bounded from a thicket. I aimed my shotgun. The distance was less than fifty yards. But it was a doe. I lowered my weapon and watched the whitetail disappear in the thick brush of the slope. I decided to finish my climb to the top anyway.

One of the beauties of hunting is the fact that I don't have to bag game to feel the time spent was worthwhile. The forest, the hills, the weather, glimpses of various birds or other wildlife—all combine to give me a sense of God's craftsmanship and diversity, and his own very real presence. It's like an ultimate worship experience, where I'm praising God for what I see and hear, while all around me animals and insects and reptiles are making music to heaven: "I heard every creature in heaven and on earth and under the earth and on the sea, and all that is in them, singing" (Revelation 5:13 NIV 1984).

I ascended a final ridge. I didn't think it was going to be my day to harvest a buck, but I stepped carefully up a trail of gravel and scree just in case. At the top was a thick bush and I came around it softly. I expected to see more bare rock. A grizzly bear, startled, gave a whoof and lifted its head from where it was feeding on a patch of clover. There was no more than twenty feet between us.

My mouth went dry. Instantly. The hairs on the back of my neck rose just as quickly and I could feel them poking against the collar of my fishing vest. Everything suddenly became walled in, and the grizzly was at one end of a short corridor and I was at another.

Saliva evaporating from your mouth. Hair standing up at the back of your neck. Tunnel vision. These were all things I'd read and heard about, but considered exaggerations. Now I was experiencing the truth of those sensations firsthand on a remote hill where I faced an eight-hundred-pound bear.

I didn't move. Neither did the grizzly. In one second, with one or two bounds, it could be on top of me. The law did not permit me to hunt a grizzly without a special tag; however, it did permit me to shoot in self-defense. But I was not holding a Holland and Holland .700 Nitro Express in my hands and had no illusions about a charge of 00 buck stopping a grizzly. It would have the same effect, Kit Carson once wrote, as grains of sand.

The bear did not take its small eyes off me. I knew that grizzlies were believed to be nearsighted. That only if I ran would I be in trouble because it would see the movement, consider me prey, and attack. But I'd also been told as a child they couldn't climb trees, and one had recently gone sixty feet up a tree in Alberta, hauled a woman down who had scaled it to get out of harm's way, and killed her.

I remained motionless. I felt that if I moved backward, it would lunge. If I dropped and rolled into a ball, it would still lunge. There was no sign of cubs in the vicinity, but that didn't mean they weren't there. They could be in the brush and frozen into immobility just like their mother.

I had never felt so trapped or confused in my life. I couldn't think of a single solution to my dilemma. It's one thing to scope a grizzly from half a mile away or watch it from your pickup. It's another to be so close you can smell the reek of its fur.

A charge could come at any second. I wouldn't survive it. Even if I turned to run, it would be on me, clamping its powerful jaws into my head or neck. If I dropped down to feign death, it would swat me with its paw before I was halfway to the ground. The six-inch claws, let alone the force of the blow, would open me up.

I felt like a man who has only a moment left to live, unless he can come up with something fast. But every plan that sprang to mind I rejected as useless or too risky. This was not a television show with a prearranged script. I really could die.

I prayed, but my prayer was very basic Sunday school stuff: *Lord, help me. I don't know what to do. There's nothing I can do. God!*

Maybe a minute went by. It could have been two. Our eyes remained locked on each other. I was not about to so much as twitch a finger, blink an eye, or move a foot in any direction. The grizzly did not shift its weight or shake its head or attempt to take a step either, but that didn't mean it couldn't change its mind in a flash, roar like a mountain wind, rush forward, and tear me apart.

Suddenly it put its head down, turned away, and moved slowly and heavily into the thicket behind it. I listened to the snapping of branches for a few moments. Then all was quiet.

I had read about bears pretending to go away, keeping an eye on their quarry, and then, when an opportunity presented itself, moving against their target with blinding speed. So I waited and watched and listened. Just because I couldn't see the bear didn't mean it couldn't see me. My turning and half running down the slope might be just the sort of activity it was hoping for.

I'm certain I remained there at least another five minutes. Then I took one step backward. The brush did not explode with a brown bear hurtling out at me, jaws wide and spewing saliva. I took another step, not daring to avert my eyes from where the grizzly had gone into the thicket, trying to feel with my boot for a safe place to bring my foot down. One more step. Then I was behind the large bush that I had rounded when I first made my way to the top.

I hesitated for several seconds, straining to hear the sounds of a big body moving fast over rock and clover. Finally, I made my way down the trail of loose stones as swiftly and safely as I could, trying not to turn my ankle or fall and crack my head against a boulder or the trunk of a tree. Once I reached the bottom, I got away from the ridge as quickly as I could and out of sight into a tangle of aspen and bushes, heading, with purpose, in the direction of my jeep.

I never felt it was over. I never relaxed, and the saliva didn't return to my mouth for the longest time. Every now and then I stopped to listen—was I being pursued? When I reached the jeep, the aftereffects of adrenaline made my hands tremble and I dropped my keys in the dirt twice. Finally, I got inside and locked the doors, staring through the windshield to see if a bear was thundering through the trees and down the logging road at thirty-five or forty miles per hour. After a few moments, I leaned my head back and closed my eyes and whispered, "Thanks."

I was afraid of the bear, though I have no idea if the bear was afraid of me. Still, in the wilderness, it watched me, saw that I meant it no harm, and permitted me to live. At the time I could not savor the experience. Now, because I was not hurt, I do. I saw a magnificent creature up close, close enough to touch, and it let me be. It was an extraordinary moment of God's grace.

There are, I suppose, all kinds of reasons the grizzly left me alone. I will never know them all and neither will anyone else. Nor will I ever understand how much of a part God played in it, not on this side of life. Perhaps there was an angel. It sounds far-fetched, but who knows? When Jesus was among the wild ones the angels were there too. "He was with the wild animals, and angels attended him" (Mark 1:13).

It could not have been coincidence that the Son of God had the wilderness animals with him. Jesus' life was not a life of coincidence. And I doubt my experience with the grizzly was a coincidence either. Do the children of God live out lives that are strings of coincidences any more than their Lord and Master? The Bible says God knew me before I was born and that he was well aware of all the days of my life before one of them came to be. So my day of the grizzly is there too (Psalm 139).

But what does it mean? I have thought about it many times and I really can't say. Except there is this—the encounter did not make me value God's creation less. Rather, its value was elevated. I did not love creation less, I loved it more. I did not return to the wilderness in fear and anxiety after the incident, but in anticipation of something greater because I had been so near one of the most powerful creatures in North America and was somehow permitted to walk away unscathed. Who knew what incredible thing might happen next?

5

Shark Attack

> There is the sea, vast and spacious, teeming with creatures beyond number—living things both large and small.
>
> Psalm 104:25

There are no sharks here, they said. Not really.

Basking sharks, sure. But they're not man-killers. Forget what you've seen in the movies. The sea is safe here.

It was my first call to a church, and it was on the east coast of Canada. I had grown up in the Canadian Midwest, just north of Minnesota and the Dakotas, and I had always longed to see two things: mountains and oceans. I traveled to the Rockies and the Pacific Ocean when I was fifteen and marveled at the sight of high blue peaks and long stretches of sparkling blue water. But the Atlantic was different—it was the rugged, gray-bearded ocean that had seen many a shipwreck, many a pirate, and many a battle between square-rigged sailing vessels flying the colors of France, Spain, England, and America. In 1912 it had seen the Titanic go down 329 miles off the coast of Newfoundland. During the Second World War, it had seen the U-boats of Germany, as well as the convoys of Canada as they steamed out of Halifax with supplies for Great Britain. The Atlantic was the Old Man of the Sea.

Nova Scotia is almost an island—only a narrow strip of land connects it to New Brunswick and the North American continent. Its shores are covered in beaches—some rocky, some sandy, some a mix of both. I often drove to beaches near the church and looked out over the sea, praying and seeking inspiration for my Sunday messages.

No man can go into the mountains or forests, no matter who he is or what he believes, and not at some point think God thoughts. The same is true of the world's oceans—you see the expansive sky and great spread of water, you hear the thunder of breaking waves and the shriek of the gull, you take in the sharp smell of seaweed and salt, you feel the spray of whitecaps and the cut of the wind. In a storm, you are overwhelmed by the power and the glory. Standing at the ocean's edge, or taking a boat onto the waves, it is impossible not to wonder about eternity and spirit and the ways of God with earth, sky, sea, and man.

One morning I opened the local paper and saw a picture I will never forget. A number of fishermen were standing on shore with a large net and smiling at the camera. Tangled in the net was a shark. The snout of the shark was unmistakable to anyone who had seen the film *Jaws*. I almost dropped the paper on the floor.

"That's a great white!" I exclaimed to the woman of the house where I was boarding.

She peered at the photograph. "It's dead."

"But it was alive before it got caught up in the net. Great whites are man-killers. I thought you said there weren't any dangerous sharks in Nova Scotia waters."

She smiled. "Now and then I suppose one or two lose their way."

The shark hadn't run into the net far out, but close to shore. Suddenly my summer swims seemed a little riskier. The last thing I wanted to see was a great white's open mouth looming up at me out of the depths as I breast-stroked a hundred yards out to a marker buoy and back. And hadn't the young woman attacked by a great white at the beginning of *Jaws* been killed while clinging to a marker buoy?

My girlfriend's father had spent his whole life on or near the Atlantic. An island boy, he'd retired early from his telecommunications position in Halifax so he could spend the rest of his working days commercial fishing for cod, halibut, haddock, and lobster. A true sea dog of his generation, he didn't know how to swim, and while his boat carried radio and sonar, it did not have any special emergency gear or flotation suits he could slip into if it began to sink.

"You're going to die anyways in that sea," he told me. "Having a flotation suit just prolongs it."

The two of us were heading out into a brass-colored dawn on his boat *White Swan* one morning when we spotted a dorsal fin and a back fin.

"What kind of shark is that?" I asked.

"Hard to say," he responded as he steered the boat. "But you can see the tail fin is a good distance from the dorsal. Could be harmless. Could be something more."

"Have you ever had a run-in with a shark?"

He grunted. "I almost lost my wife to one."

It had been a day like today, my girlfriend's father told me, bright and clear, and he and his wife were heading out

49

together for a day's fishing. He used his sonar, but he also tracked what the gulls were doing and visited some of his favorite spots, like any good fisherman would. They were using handlines, basically just long spools of line with a number of baited hooks dangling at the end. They'd caught a decent number of cod by noon, but what excited both of them most was the number of haddock they'd caught (at the time, scarce). They let the engine idle and had lines over both sides as they bit into the sandwiches his wife had prepared and drank down bottles of cold juice.

They were in the open ocean—the coasts of Maine and Massachusetts were a few hundred nautical miles to the west, and the coasts of Spain and France a few thousand nautical miles to the east. After they'd finished their lunch, they brought up their handlines and steered the *White Swan* to a new location, where they re-baited the hooks and let them down into the Atlantic again. He turned to check on the engine and their coordinates, glancing at the sonar screen while she busied herself putting more lines over the side. Sun and shadow swept quickly over the face of the sea.

Her scream made him snap up his head from the sonar— she was being dragged across the deck and over the side of the boat. A hook had imbedded itself in her arm and the line was being yanked into the water with fierce strength. He ran to her, jerking a knife from its sheath on his belt. A monstrous head, mouth gaping and sharp teeth gleaming, was rising up through the sea, swallowing the hooks and bait as it came. He could not fight it and he could not hold her back as she slipped over the edge. With a swift and powerful movement he chopped down at the line as it stretched over the hull. It broke and she tumbled back into the boat. The shark's head emerged, snapped at the end of the line and the air, then rolled and dropped back into the deep.

He held and comforted his wife and told her he needed to use the knife to cut the hook free. Slicing into her skin, he found the hook, removed the barb, and drew the hook from her arm. Then he grabbed the first aid kit and cleaned the wound with water and antiseptic and wrapped it in gauze.

"We'll head in," he said. "That's enough excitement for the day."

"I'm so sorry," she replied. "I was working with the lines and suddenly one of them leaped up and a hook flew into my arm before I could do anything."

"He'd gotten ahold of the bait and was biting down. It wasn't your fault. I just thank God you're okay."

"Yes, thank God—and thank you."

As he told me this story, the boat was running through a sea as calm as a pond, light flashing off its surface as the sun rose fully into the sky.

"It was just like this here," he said. "No different."

"Hard to believe when it looks so beautiful," I responded.

He turned the wheel of the boat deftly in his hands. "There's no telling out on the blue water. There's no telling what's under your feet."

As we continued I brought the handlines out of the locker, along with the bait, and began to prepare them for going over the side when he found the fishing spot he wanted.

I remembered a sentence from Herman Melville's *Moby Dick* as the boat slipped through the quiet morning sea:

These are the times of dreamy quietude, when beholding the tranquil beauty and brilliancy of the ocean's skin, one forgets the tiger heart that pants beneath it; and would not willingly remember, that this velvet paw but conceals a remorseless fang.[1]

1. Herman Melville, *Moby Dick or The Whale* (New York: Charles Scribner's Sons, 1902), 422.

The Bible tells us many stories of man and water—the Flood, Noah and the ark, Jonah being swallowed by a great fish or whale, the disciples casting their nets into the Sea of Galilee, Jesus walking on the waves. The sea has as many creatures and wonders as the mountains and dry land.

"Those who go down to the sea in ships," the Bible tells us, "who do business on great waters; they have seen the works of the Lord, and his wonders in the deep" (Psalm 107:23–24 NASB).

In the same way forests and streams inspire awe and direct our thoughts to the Creator, so do vast oceans, lakes, and inland seas. Salt water and fresh water bless as much as valleys and hills. Sunrise and sunset over the Atlantic and Pacific inspire and make a man glad to be alive.

As some hike on land, others swim in the sea. As some hunt on land, others hunt on the sea. As some photograph wildlife on land and are astonished at the power and beauty of the animals and birds, others photograph in and around the great waters and are stunned by the strength and beauty of the wild creatures that live on its shores and in its depths. "So is this great and wide sea, wherein are things creeping innumerable, both small and great beasts" (Psalm 104:25 KJV).

The wildness of the oceans has as much ability to bring men closer to God and who they are as the wildness of peaks and woods.

This is God's world and it is beautiful in so many ways. Yet the seas, just like the wilderness on land, have been twisted by man's fall from grace and marred by a terrible brokenness, so that while waves can soothe, they can also drown a man; while marlins and dolphins are startling in their grace and intelligence, other sea creatures can kill with poison or with teeth.

When a man goes into the mountains and forests, or out upon the vast waters, he does so with gratitude for the greatness that has not been lost and for the adventure that is his to enjoy. Yet he also does so in readiness to meet whatever dangers and adversity come his way. And, like my wife's father, he does so with courage, faith, and all that he has learned of the ways and means of surviving the wild, violent, but still magnificent spaces of earth and sea.

6

The Swimming Moose

If you lay a hand on it, you will remember the
struggle and never do it again!

Job 41:8

There is nothing necessarily unusual or upsetting about a
moose swimming. They are strong swimmers, which comes
in handy in the swamps and wetlands where they love to feed.
The problem is when they swim straight at you and emerge
dripping wet with murder in their eyes—that's unusual and
upsetting.

My son, Micah, and I had gone for an evening picnic at
a mountain lake not far from our home. He was four at the
time. My wife and I took our son and daughter into the wilderness from the time they were born. Long before my boy
could walk he was going up mountainsides in a baby carrier,
picking huckleberries as I held him in my arms, or traversing
swift mountain streams riding on my shoulders. When his

sister, Micaela, was eight, and he was about to enter double digits, we sat down and made a list and figured out they had seen more wildlife (out in the wild) in ten years than I had seen in my first twenty-one years of life.

You take a few risks bringing your kids into untamed wilderness. On the other hand, you also take certain risks sending them to school or camp or any number of other places. We take risks with our children all the time because we believe the benefits of taking them to a fireworks display or an indoor pool or encouraging them to get into football or hockey or Tae Kwon Do will outweigh the risks. The same applies in showing them the high peaks and vast grasslands and towering evergreen forests—we believe the things they see and experience in God's creation will benefit them for a lifetime, justifying any risks.

But like the rest of life, you don't know when the wilderness might shift from peace to storm mode in the blink of an eye. So when I took my very young and enthusiastic son to the lake and we spread out our "guy eats" on a picnic table, I had one eye on him and one on the wilderness forest not a hundred yards away. Happily he dumped out our bag— big chunks of cheese and sausage, jars of peanut butter and jelly, a loaf of bread, raw carrots, beef jerky, cookies, milk, Coke—all six basic food groups. We laughed and talked and ate with gusto as we prepared for a walk around the small lake after our meal.

The trouble began with a barking dog. There's nothing odd about a barking dog—except in a wilderness area they need to be on a leash. We looked up from our feast and saw him running around on the opposite side of the lake. The dog was loose, the master was chasing the dog, and the dog was chasing a bull moose. If there had been a ranger or a wildlife officer present, the dog would have been impounded and the master arrested and fined. But no one was there to help the moose. So it plunged into the lake to get away.

To my shock the dog leaped right in after it. The master did nothing but call his dog's name over and over again just as he had been doing all along—"Sammy! Sammy!" And just as the dog had been doing all along, he ignored his master's shouts. Sammy paddled madly after the moose and the moose paddled madly for the shore—our shore.

At first it looked like the moose was going to veer to its right and make landfall sooner rather than later. But it changed its mind and came straight for me and my son. Our Jeep Cherokee was hundreds of yards away in the parking lot. I considered running with my boy in my arms, but I knew a moose could run fast, very fast—much faster than I could run carrying a four-year-old.

The whole thing was crazy. How had the dog owner let this situation develop in the first place? Why hadn't he raced after his dog and snapped the leash on his collar? All he'd done was walk and call—never shout—the dog's name, acting as if it was no big deal and he was in complete control of the situation. Now with his dog swimming after the moose, he chose not to jump in himself but walk—not run!—around the lake to meet him on the other side. The dog and moose were going to be at our picnic table long before the dog owner got there.

You know those times you wish you could whip out a flashing red light, put it on your dash, and pull over some crazy driver on the freeway? Or jam a green cap on your head that says US Border Patrol and walk into a crowded and noisy room and watch everyone vanish out every door they could find? Right then I wanted a Park Ranger Stetson very badly.

But all I could do was put my son on top of the picnic table, jump up after him, and hold him in my arms. The moose hit the shore with a roar, swinging its head and glaring white-eyed all around, its huge antlers spraying drops of water like rain. The dog came ashore on its heels and lunged. The moose had had enough. It held its ground and charged. The startled dog began to run backward as fast as he could, still barking to show, like his master a half mile away, that he was in control, despite appearances to the contrary.

The moose kept coming and the dog kept running. Now the dog wanted his master and bolted in that general direction. The moose let him go, snorted like a peal of thunder, and turned to glare wild-eyed at us. Standing on the picnic table made me and my son taller than he was, but he wasn't impressed. He came toward us baring his teeth and flattening his ears. He could easily reach us with those teeth and antlers, sweep us to the ground, and strike with hooves that carried a half ton of power behind them.

After a deadly moose incident I'd experienced the year before, an RCMP friend had told me crews that work in the bush often carry long steel poles with them. These poles are solely for the purpose of facing down a bull moose in a bad temper. It's all about rack size and once the person thrusts the pole above their head the bull moose snorts, stares, and backs down—the size of the antlers means his opponent is far too large to contemplate taking on in a fight. It was all I could think of doing now. I had no pole, but I had one free arm and I was already standing ten feet tall. I threw my arm high over my head.

The moose snorted, swung its head from side to side, and began to step backward. It glanced around at the dog—Sammy was barking again but was now attached firmly to its leash and being led away by its master. Still not in the best of humor, the moose threw back its head and antlers and trotted off toward the woods while I kept my arm over my head. In moments, it crashed through the first pines and disappeared, though I could hear it making its way by the cracking of branches. I let my hand drop. But I didn't come down off the table with my son for at least five more minutes, wanting to be sure the moose really had left us alone. Then we gathered up our food and made our way quickly to the Cherokee.

"You okay?" I asked my boy.

Micah nodded with a serious look on his young face. "That wasn't fair to the moose."

"You mean the dog chasing it? No, it wasn't. But no one got hurt, thank goodness—not us, not the moose, not the dog."

"I prayed—did you?"

"I did, son."

"Can we finish our picnic, Dad?"

"You bet," I said. "Where would you like to eat?"

He gave me a small smile. "Is it okay if we finish our picnic in the jeep?"

I laughed. "It sure is okay. And it's a very guy thing too."

"Good," he said. "I want to start with the cookies in case we run out of time again."

"Go right ahead."

When we had finished cookies and Coke and carrots and sausage and everything else, he said to me, "A wilderness picnic is good inside a truck. But I'm glad we were outside to start with and saw the moose."

Despite its dangers, God's wilderness has an enduring appeal for all ages and generations. Men and boys—and women and girls—consider the risks worth the blessing gained to be among God's trees and mountains, as well as his deer and bear and elk and moose.

7

Mother Bear's Climbing Lesson

Can you bring forth the constellations in their
seasons or lead out the Bear with its cubs?

Job 38:32

I always have a hard time figuring out how the constellations
Ursa Major and Ursa Minor, Great Bear and Little Bear, actually look like bears even after I connect the dots. I have no
such trouble in the wild places—there a grizzly looks like a
grizzly, and black bears (which can also be brown), look like
black bears, cubs look like cubs, and mother bears definitely
look and act like mothers who need no advice on how to go
about protecting their young.

It was a stormy Sunday afternoon when I piled Yukon and
Nahanni into the Cherokee and took off for a walk in the
forest. Rain is not a great thing if it catches you out hiking,
and it's even less inviting if it goes on for days and you are
stuck with too many others in too small a tent. But you can

enjoy rain in God's country when you have a warm home or cabin to return to. The dogs and I didn't mind if we got soaked because there was a house waiting for us at the end of the day.

It wasn't a driving rain at all. It was a slow and quiet rain that hung on pine and spruce needles like little round mirrors—you could see your reflection in them and the reflection of the trees behind you. A mist hung about the forest too, as if the woods had breath that came out white in the cool air. A wild place in the wet isn't the same as a wild place sunny and dry. The atmosphere is altogether different. There is a hush, the birds are not calling, very little seems to be moving, everything is waiting for the rain to finish its work.

We became as subdued as the forest and its creatures. The dogs padded silently on the ends of their leashes as I walked softly behind. We could hear a creek rushing over stones far away and the water dripping from leaves and needles. The woods during a long rain are a gift from God, custom made for deep thought, for turning things over in your mind, for prayer, and for a worship of God that is personal and profound. Truth be told, I was feeling a little low and hoped the mix of dogs and wilderness and storm might pick me up.

Like too many of God's gifts, a storm is seldom enjoyed because we wait for the rain to stop before venturing out-of-doors. The rainfall is seen as a nuisance or inconvenience to our plans when, in fact, its beauty can offer us rare experiences if only we enter into it. Unfortunately, we withdraw from many of life's trials and challenges which could be transforming if properly embraced.

Since the quiet was so intense, anything that did make a sound was instantly noticeable. Both dogs pricked up their ears when there was a sudden scraping like fingernails being drawn over rough wood. We stopped and tried to figure the noise out. Their heads were cocked. The scraping was long and drawn out, lasting several seconds. In unspoken consent we began to move toward it, taking several different trails as we did so. Each time we stopped to listen we heard it again—scraa-aa-aape, scraa-aa-aape—the sound growing louder and louder as we approached.

Suddenly the dogs stopped and stared into the under-growth. I turned my head and saw a bear cub trying to climb a tree and failing. Its small claws were dug in and as the cub slid back down they made the long scraping sound the dogs and I had puzzled over. As I watched the cub slip downward, I noticed another one on a different tree trunk trying to suc-ceed where the first had failed. Up it climbed, digging in as best it could, but it could not keep its grip and, just like the other cub, began to slide down, still trying to grasp the tree, its paws making the rasping sound of tiny claws on bark.

It was fascinating to watch the cubs try to climb up the trunks. The dogs did not growl or make any sound at all. They seemed as mesmerized as I! But a new sound mingled with the scraping noise—whimpering. With a start, I real-ized the bear cubs, scarcely fifty feet away, were frightened of us. I had been so caught up in their attempts to scale the tall trees I hadn't even considered the effect of our arrival. This no sooner dawned on me than I wondered: *But where is the mother bear? Has something happened to her? Are they scared because they are all alone?*

The thought barely had time to form in my mind before a massive black head, speckled with silver raindrops, came up out of the brush and dark eyes stared directly at us. I caught my breath—Ursa Major, Great Bear. I was sure she was going to attack.

The cubs may have been whimpering, but I was the one who was frightened now. Judging by the head and shoulders that I could see, the mother was huge. In a mixture of relief that the cubs were not orphans and panic that she could be on us in one bound, I immediately turned the dogs around and headed back the way we had come, walking swiftly. I thanked God the mother did not come charging after us.

But then I heard the unmistakable sounds of a big creature crashing just as swiftly through the forest beside us, parallel to our route. The three bears were getting out of the area too and obviously trying to put distance between themselves and us. The trouble was our path was about to take a sharp turn to the left—we would run into each other again, only this time we would be face-to-face.

I hoped we might still have a chance to avoid a collision and pulled back on the dogs' leashes. At the same time, Nahanni, a grumpy look on her lean coyote face, glared toward the forest where the noise was coming from and gave a loud bark of warning, the first time either of the dogs had made a sound. The crashing in the woods stopped immediately. I waited. There was no more noise or movement. Obviously alarmed to discover we were right on top of them again, the mother bear and her brood were rooted to the spot, showing no indication of heading forward until they knew we were gone.

I obliged them. After several long seconds of silence from the bears, I started the dogs at a half run, taking the turn and rushing past where the mother and cubs had hunkered down. I still thought she might roar out of the bush and lunge at us—she may not have been a grizzly, but black bears have attacked and mauled people and their dogs too. Soon, my half run became a full run. Yukon and Nahanni loved it, thinking it was a great adventure, stretching out beside and ahead of me, their long legs a blur. I wanted to get as far away as rapidly as possible and they were happy to help me do just that.

After several minutes we fell back to a fast walk. The forest was green and silent and misty once more. There were no sounds of breaking branches. The rain draped us in a shower of fine silver drops. Soaked, spooked, but not just a little exhilarated to come away safely from such an astonishing encounter, I opened the back of the jeep for the dogs to leap in and climbed behind the wheel.

"That's not something you see every day," I said to them. "Thanks for getting me out walking in all kinds of weather and in all kinds of places."

They stared out the windows hoping to see more excitement coming at them. But the forest kept the rest of her secrets that day. I turned the key in the ignition, almost hating to disrupt the pristine green and silver stillness. We headed to the house for towels and warmth and Sunday dinner. That night the weather broke, the clouds pulled apart, and the sky gleamed with ten thousand stars. The Bear and its cubs were easy to make out in all their dark and sparkling beauty.

I've never seen anything like it since. And never been that close to a mother bear and her cubs again. I thanked God for the experience we'd had by going out into the storm to see what we could find, rather than simply staying indoors, avoiding the wind and rain.

8

The Mountain Lion
and the Winchester 94

There are three things that are stately in their
stride, four that move with stately bearing: a
lion, mighty among beasts, who retreats before
nothing. . . .

Proverbs 30:29–30

The densest population of mountain lions or cougars in
North America is on Vancouver Island. We lived there for
five years and both our children were born on the Island. Yet
I only saw the great cat twice—one time, perched high up a
tree, staring down at my dogs and me, and the other, striding
at the edge of my property as if it owned the land, glaring
fixedly at me as if I were the intruder.

The part of the Island we lived in sees an average of 121
inches of rain a year—that's over ten feet of water. The
north and west see even more. Most of this falls in the winter

months, but all the other seasons can see a fair amount of rain too. Things grow fast and strong on the Island, no matter what you plant. That includes the trees, especially the cedars, which grow tall and thick and create a rain forest that in places is almost impenetrable. Old bones are still found of sailors, shipwrecked on the Island's Pacific coast, who tried to make their way through the heavily forested interior to the city of Victoria on the southern tip. The Island is a jungle, which is why the mountain lion loves it, and most of the people live in coastal communities that ring the deep, dark woods which cover ninety percent of the land.

Because of the rain, you find yourself mowing the lawn all year round. So if you don't have to shovel it (a popular Island saying which means you don't have to shovel snow because it's all rainwater) you do have to cut it, sometimes twice a week in the spring and summer. It so happened one June that I had been busy as a pastor, father, husband, writer, and dog walker. The lawn had been neglected and the problem with such neglect is the grass seems to grow a foot a week—if you let it go too long your yard literally becomes a hayfield. Our lawn was rapidly becoming that hayfield. So I made the time and got out the power mower and prepared to tackle a yard that wanted to revert to a rain forest.

But it is not only human busyness that keeps grass from getting cut promptly on the Island. There's the rain that never really goes away. You might be free to mow the lawn, but the rain will fall and not let you do it. My determination made no difference to the Pacific storm systems. Again and again, I had to put good intentions and my mower back in the garage. Eventually, there was a break in the rainfall. I had time on my hands. With steely determination to cut the lawn, no matter what happened, I began to mow. Hack might be a better term if you can imagine a mower being wielded like a machete—I often had to rear it up on its back wheels and drop it down with a thump on the tall grass to get anywhere without clogging the blades and stalling the engine. Nevertheless, I was making progress for the first time in weeks when a car came racing up, the driver leaning on the horn and thrusting her head out of the window.

"I just saw a mountain lion walk down the middle of the street in front of our house," she said. "We live one block over. I followed it in my car and it came this way. It's on your property. You'd better get indoors. I've got to tell the other neighbors."

I watched her go, startled. Glancing at the line of bushes that separated our yard from a small farm, I didn't see any lion, so I kept cutting. It wasn't that I didn't believe her—the cats came into Island communities all the time, stalking deer and pets. It's just that I had had it with delays and I was going to keep cutting while I had the chance.

My wife came to the back door. "Hey. A neighbor just called. There have been cougar sightings—at the farm next door and in the bushes between their house and ours. Maybe you'd better park the mower for now."

"I can't," I said over the roar of the machine.

"Why can't you?"

"I have to finish this."

"It's a mountain lion."

"Put the dogs in for me, will you? And keep the kids indoors."

"But what about you?"

I shook my head and kept cutting.

In a few minutes, the only ones out and about in my neighborhood were a woman doing something with her apple tree and a man who actually felt he needed to water his lawn with a hose. I doubted the lion would do anything to me or the other two when it had plenty of deer to hunt. Being a stealthy predator, I also doubted it would ever show itself. The sun was out, I was making some real headway, and I was determined to keep going.

It was when I came near the line of thick brush that grew between our property and the farm that I saw the face in the shadows. I was sure I had imagined it because the next moment the face was gone. Then I saw the long tawny body, walking in that insolent way even house cats have through the screen of leaves and branches.

Suddenly the cat came out into the open and stared at me, its impossibly long tail twitching slowly. In a moment the cat vanished again. It happened so quickly part of me was sure I had seen the lion while another part of me was just as sure I hadn't. I turned off the mower. The silence was loud. I stared at the bushes but couldn't see any movement. I made up my mind, went in the house, grabbed a Winchester 94, and took it outside with me.

"What are you going to do?" my wife called after me. "Are you going to shoot it?"

"I don't know."

"But that old rifle doesn't even work anymore. You took the firing pin out."

"Maybe the cat knows what a gun looks like."

"What are you talking about?"

"I read somewhere that animals can smell guns. I always keep it well oiled."

I propped the Winchester up against the house so that if the cat was still in the bushes it could see the lever-action carbine was there. I really *had* read about the ability of animals to scent gunmetal and oil and to recognize the shape of a firearm and react accordingly—either to take immediate flight or launch an immediate attack. There were better rifles in my gun safe, ones that actually fired, and for which

I had the ammunition. But I didn't want to take the time to find the keys, open the safe, get a gun, lock it back up, then hunt out the ammo locker, get the key for that, find a box of cartridges, load the weapon, and finally head back outside. So the wall hanger gun became my means of defense just on looks and smell alone.

The cat was nowhere to be seen. I was being a bit reckless. I knew lions had gone after adults as well as children, but at the same time I wasn't being that reckless because I also knew most lions didn't do anything to humans. Why stalk me when the nearby woods were full of bucks and does? I started the mower with two yanks.

I couldn't see any movement in the bushes, there was no whiskered face in the shadows, no more neighbors raced down the street in their cars to warn me a lion was still slinking around the edges of my property. The sun shone, I kept cutting, and an hour later the long job was finished. I didn't see the mountain lion again, there were no more warnings, and I never heard that a cougar made a kill in the neighborhood that day or any day afterward.

If you don't live in cougar country, my stubborn actions may seem immature and over the top. But the truth is if you stopped your work in places like Vancouver Island every time there was a cougar sighting, a lot of things would never get done. You take precautions and, like the man watering his lawn or the woman with her apple tree, you carry on. A person knows the highway is dangerous, he knows there was a fatal accident on his route the day before, but he gets in his car, fastens his seatbelt, and drives to work anyway—what else is he supposed to do?

A woman climbs on board a plane to get to her dying father as quickly as possible, even though she knows planes go down and people get killed a dozen times every year—what else can she do if she wants to see her father while he's still alive? All of us take risks and get on with our lives on a daily basis. Living in cougar country is no different—and a lot more people are killed in traffic accidents or in air disasters than are killed by mountain lions.

You have to have a lot of courage to make it in this world. You have to have the heart of a lion. It is not by chance that the Bible constantly refers to the lion as an example of fearlessness, and we all need that sort of spirit to face the challenges of life, large and small. Being fed up and determined to finish your yard work is a simple matter, even with a mountain lion who has dared to come down out of the wild forests.

Facing prostate cancer is something else entirely. Or dealing with heart disease. Or losing your legs in an IED blast on the outskirts of Kandahar. Or coming to grips with the sudden death of a close friend, your mother, your daughter, or your son.

We need to ask God for the heart that is in that mighty lion, who retreats from nothing but faces everything. We need to pray for the fearless heart that is in the Lion of the tribe of Judah, Jesus Christ himself. It's true that those who believe have that heart already, but like the physical heart, it's a matter of keeping our spiritual hearts strong by putting them to use. We need to take on the spiritual challenges and barriers and overcome them. When we do, this verse becomes true for us: "The wicked flee when no man pursueth: but the righteous are bold as a lion" (Proverbs 28:1 KJV).

9

Fly-Fishing With Grizzlies

He was unto me as a bear lying in wait, and as a
lion in secret places.

Lamentations 3:10 KJV

I will meet them as a bear that is bereaved of her
[cubs], and will rend the caul of their heart.

Hosea 13:8 KJV

While the hunter or hiker or backcountry camper may seem to
be most at risk in grizzly country, often it is the fly-fisherman,
who moves silently along the banks of trout streams with
deep forests behind him, that surprises the great bear under
circumstances that can swiftly turn lethal.

Southwestern Alberta, like western Montana just below
it, is a paradise of mountain streams and fast rivers where
trout of all kind live and thrive. For the fly-fisherman, the
roar is not of a boat engine on a lake, but a waterfall rushing

over rocks thousands of years old. People do not talk to him, for he works alone, and if there is a partner he is far off and silent and carrying on his own conversation with God and creation. The man that fly-fishes does not mind the absence of other humans or of being in a world that consists only of water, rock, and shafts of light. He is content in wilderness places where men or women are rarely seen and he can work his long fly rod with an easy rhythm and grace, lose himself, and be healed by the God-made mountains and waters. Even the man who says there is no God feels the tug on his heart and goes deep into the wild places for a touch of the divine that he often calls something else.

People come from all over the world to fly-fish these waters. They hire a guide and set off to find waterways that are like blue veins upon the earth. There they can find rest for their souls, if they wish it, not only by standing within the masterworks of the Master Craftsman, but by daring to reach out for the Master himself. For that too they may need a guide, though for some the way to Christ is already known if not always taken.

With all those men and women fishing the fast waters, it is a wonder more are not harmed by crossing paths with bears, who also like the lonely places and cold waters and leaping fish. For while we live on this earth and tread its wilderness ways, there is always the beauty and always the beast, always great peace and great danger. Still, it shocked me to pick up the local paper one summer morning and see, not as the main headline, but in a column to the side, a story that began with the header "Grizzly Kills Man."

Yes, more die on American and Canadian highways each summer than are ever mauled or killed by grizzlies. More die of lung cancer or heart disease. But there is something painful about a man or woman going into the wilderness to enjoy its grandeur and freedom and dying violently there in the midst of that joy.

The man in the story was fly-fishing. The weather was good, the fish plentiful. He was camping with some friends and had gone off alone to try his luck. When he was gone far longer than seemed right, even for an avid fisherman, one of them went to investigate.

He found his friend dead, partially eaten and half buried under leaves and debris. His shock and grief must have been overwhelming. It was unclear to me whether he had a firearm with him and, finding the grizzly lurking by the body, shot the bear on sight. Or whether he went back to the campsite, got a gun, returned to find the grizzly hovering over its kill, and shot the bear dead then. But his reaction is understandable, and he was not charged by wildlife officials, even though the grizzly is a protected animal.

Whenever someone is killed by a bear, or another animal, that bear or animal is normally hunted down and harvested. There is always debate over this. Increasingly people side with the animals, arguing that being on their turf changes the rules. Unless you have a rogue proven to have killed other humans, the animal should be left alone. Others maintain that if it can't be shown that the human provoked the animal it must be hunted down and dispatched to keep it from taking other human lives. This is what makes the other bear attack that occurred that summer take on different proportions.

The man was fly-fishing alone, walking quietly on the bank and in the waters, casting his line carefully into the nooks and crannies of the river. No friends were waiting for him back at his truck. He had come up into the mountains by himself to be totally immersed in its splendor and secrets. How softly did he move? So softly the mother grizzly never heard him. That is how much he valued the stillness.

When she finally did scent him and spot his movement she realized instantly he had come between her and her cubs. Of course the man had not meant to. He had no idea she and her cubs were there. But the grizzly sow did not know that. She could never know that. In a fury she exploded out of the brush and launched herself at him. He had no chance to run and she tore him apart.

The man feigned death on the riverbank. After she had finished swatting him with her six-inch claws and biting him with her four-inch fangs, satisfied he no longer posed a threat to her young, she hustled her cubs out of the area and disappeared. He was bleeding from dozens of wounds, in such shock that he did not yet feel the full extent of the pain of his injuries. Knowing he had to get help fast before he passed out, he still waited to be sure the grizzly was not hiding a few feet away, watching to see if he moved and was still a danger to her young. Then he slowly got up.

Stumbling through the forest, and finally making his way to his truck, he got behind the wheel and realized he could barely see to drive. He had only one eye. And it was dangling by a few nerves. The other socket was empty. Putting his head at an angle that permitted his eye to see where he was going, he began to drive toward the nearest town. It took some time. Finally he pulled up by the gas pumps at the general store and staggered through the door.

They all knew him. He was a local. He had been in and out of the store a thousand times. But when he stumbled into their arms, his face a clot of blood, no one knew who he was. When he rasped out his name they were stunned. In moments they had him in one of their trucks and were racing for the nearest hospital, a twenty-minute drive they did in much less, holding his hands and telling him to hang on.

He lived. Over weeks and months he endured dozens of operations to repair the bones and flesh and muscle of his face and body. From the beginning of the ordeal he told the wildlife officers again and again that the incident had been his fault; he had been too quiet and the grizzly had been frightened and angered by his sudden appearance. He argued that he should have known better. The bear only responded in the way a mother bear was built by nature to respond when she felt her cubs were in danger.

"Don't shoot her," he pleaded. "She's not a man-killer. She was just protecting her babies the same as any human would. Let her live. Let her raise her cubs. Let her remain in the mountains. Don't harm her. Please."

The wildlife officials listened to him and did not take the bear down, though others say they went out and harvested the bear anyway, to be on the safe side.

The man's passion for the bear and her cubs is not something strange to hunters or fly-fishermen or anyone who loves nature and God's creation. For such people know there is a time to hunt and a time to put the rifle back on the rack, a time to harvest game and a time to let them be, a time to kill and a time to preserve, a time to avoid contact and intrusion and to let the fish and animals thrive and flourish—a time to make every effort to keep the wilderness wild. It is no wonder that those who hike or hunt or fish in the vast forests and hills, far from cities and towns, are more often than not the leaders in establishing and maintaining conservation efforts and societies. For they know that when the bear is gone, and the cougar, the Canada goose, the trout, and mallard, a whole wild world is gone forever, and a part of their hearts and souls and freedom are gone with it. Might this ultimately limit their ability to walk with the Creator of it all, get to know him, and forge a friendship that lasts longer than a lifetime?

10

Jay Jack and the Bear

Let a man meet a she-bear robbed of her cubs
rather than a fool in his folly.

Proverbs 17:12 ESV

Sometimes I wonder which is worse when I'm out in the
wilderness—man or beast.

I was single and young and had taken a summer job as a
reporter with a weekly newspaper in northern Manitoba, a
rugged land of sprawling lakes and pine forests and swamps.
The town was not that many miles from Churchill, a famous
spot for those wishing to observe and photograph the mighty
polar bear. There were no polar bears where I was, but I soon
found out there were other things to worry about.

How I ended up with Jay Jack is a mystery to me, even to
this day. I wasn't doing a story on him and he wasn't the kind
of guy I normally hung around with—sullen, silent, skinny
as a cat tail, with a greasy ball cap that advertised some

sort of power tool crammed down on his narrow head, eyes small, black, and unhappy behind his extra thick glasses. But there we were—camping together one weekend and catching walleye by the boatload in a pristine northern Canadian lake.

It was a sloppy camp. Not by my choice, but by Jay Jack's design. Food wasn't stored in lockers or in the GMC truck; it was placed under a tarp and some was even stacked inside the tent we slept in. Cans and bottles of Coke or water or juice were left out on a crude table that served both for cleaning fish and eating our meals. I didn't like the look or the smell of the camp, and I knew it wasn't a good idea to leave food out in the open in bear country. Bringing this to Jay Jack's attention made no difference, however. He brushed off my concerns as he readied our powerboat for another day's fishing.

"You worry too much, kid," he growled. "You city boys come up north with crazy ideas of spick-and-span campsites and home-cooked meals and wild animals ready to sink their fangs in your leg. I been fishing here most of my life, and keeping camp the same way we're keeping it this weekend, and nothing's ever happened. Now, get your rod and let's get to work."

Far out on the lake, the walleye continued to bite. Sometimes we latched onto a northern pike and had a battle on our hands—for that fish is a fighter and a pleasure to tangle with—but mostly we wanted walleye, the better meal of the two. Pike can be tasty, but it has a lot of bones and you have to be extra patient and fillet it just right or you're always picking something out of your teeth or worse, your throat. Sunday afternoon, we headed in with a good amount to take home, or in my case, to the British family I boarded with.

But even before we beached the small aluminum craft Jay Jack began to mutter and growl—something was amiss. We could see the blue tarp that covered our supplies had been shredded and torn down. Cartons had been ripped open and cans punctured and strewn about the camp. Our table was awash with milk and Coke and orange juice. The tent didn't even exist—there was no tent, it looked like there never had been a tent—and the pillows and sleeping bags that used to be inside it were slashed and scattered in a flutter of fabric and feathers that mixed with the apples, carrots, and potatoes Jay Jack had placed by our feet as we slept. A black bear lifted its head from the mess at the sound of the boat's engine, looked hard at us, and lit out for the woods.

Jay Jack howled and cut the engine, leaping from the boat into about four feet of water. Yelling and sputtering, and using more words than I'd heard from him for the past three days, he staggered through the water and onto shore. He ran for his truck. He threw open the back, yanked out a pump shotgun, and, fumbling with a box of shells, chased after the bear into the pine trees, letting out a sound from his throat like a baying hound. There was a gun blast. Then another. The snapping of twigs and branches, a shout, more crashing and snapping—Jay Jack did not return.

The bear hadn't been huge, but it hadn't been small either, and it was still a bear. Where was it? Had Jay missed it? Or wounded it? Was it circling around to get on his back trail like hunted bears sometimes did?

And what about Jay Jack? He was a swirling ball of fury. The bear had trashed our camp and ruined our food and gear, and Jay was going to make the bear pay by killing it. But what sort of hunter was he? How accurate was he with a shotgun? If the bear headed back this way, would Jay remember I was also in the area, or would he fire indiscriminately, figuring it was up to me to be smart enough to lie low?

Which was more dangerous—the frightened or wounded black bear or the enraged Jay Jack?

I wasn't sure. So I picked up two hatchets, one in either fist, and put myself against a pine tree, the thickest I could spot at a moment's glance. The tree was to protect my back from Jay's shotgun shells. The hatchets were to protect me from the bear. It was all I had to work with and it was all I could think of to do. Maybe I should have climbed into the truck. But I imagined shotgun pellets shattering the windshield. I stayed put, hoping I was out of harm's way.

I waited. Was the bear alive? Was it coming this way, Jay hot on its heels? Had it run deeper into a forest that stretched for hundreds of miles? Or had it turned on Jay and split his head in two? I cringed against the tree. The silence of the wild places can be wonderful, even inspiring, when you feel strong and secure in your situation. When you don't, it has a spirit of menace about it—you feel like something is going to burst out of the long green darkness with its jaws wide open.

I heard movement—the swaying of evergreen branches, the pop of twigs underfoot—and Jay emerged from the forest with his shotgun clutched in his hands like a club. His face was like some sort of voodoo mask etched in lines of hate. He scooped up a six-pack of Fresca cans and hurled it into the lake. Before it had a chance to sink, with yet another bellow of rage that boomed across the water, he fired at the green cans again and again, spray and soft drink exploding in the air, the shotgun blasts crashing through the trees. When he was done, and the cans were all destroyed, he turned to look at me and at the campsite.

"What are the hatchets for?" he growled.

"I . . . uh . . . thought I'd start cleaning up," I told him.

"Ain't much worth saving. Anything that isn't wrecked you can throw in the back of the Jimmy. The rest goes in the fire pit."

Most of our gear and food went up in flames. Once the blaze had died down to coals, Jay Jack drove back to town with what we had left, mostly a good haul of walleye, our rods, and the clothes on our backs. When he was close to dropping me off, I finally got up the nerve to ask him what had happened to the bear.

"Dunno," he grunted.

"Did you . . . did you shoot it?"

"No. He got away." He glared at me with his small black eyes. "On a full stomach. He had quite a party at our expense. Quite a party."

And I had quite an experience. I was eighteen when I had my moment with Jay Jack and the bear. From that time on I have never put food in my tent in bear country, never stored cans and bottles and cartons under a tarp, never left meat and drink sitting on a table, never cleaned fish in camp—and always chosen my hunting, fishing, and camping partners wisely. The wild that God has given us is wild enough on its own without adding wild men to the mix.

In some respects, as we are advised in Proverbs, it might be better to deal with a raging mother grizzly than a raging gun-wielding human. With proper care and respect for the wilderness and its creatures, a man or woman can go into the deep forests and come out unscathed, bear or no bear. An unpredictable human at your side, with a chip on his shoulder and an attitude as dark as a moonless night, is something else again. Thanks to Jay Jack, I learned early on I can handle God's wild better on its own terms, regardless of the hazards. If you include a rogue human element, especially one that is more rogue and unpredictable than most, it just increases the dangers without adding to the blessings one bit.

11

Deer Trails

As the deer pants for streams of water, so my soul
pants for you, my God.

Psalm 42:1

I called the mule deer Salty not only because he liked the trail
mix I left for him on the ground, but because he had a strong
thirst—and not from the mix, because the first thing he did
was drink water from a wide mouth Nalgene bottle sitting
on a rock with its top off.

My wife and I weren't in a park and we certainly weren't
on the well-worn path of a hike route. This was the Pacific
Crest Trail, a string of connected trails that runs all the way
from Canada to Mexico. We were in Washington State and
breaking camp after a short night's sleep. The deer emerged
from the brush bit by bit, headed for the bottle, and licked
up the water in it. Then he watched us chewing trail mix for
breakfast. Moving slowly, I decided to pour a handful on the

dirt not far from the rock where he had drunk from the Nalgene bottle. He backed away and then returned, cautiously approached the nuts and raisins, sniffed, and gobbled them up. I gave him three handfuls, then extended my hand with a fourth. Salty would come close but always stamped his feet like a horse at the last minute and shook his head and balked—he would not take the trail mix from my hand no matter how badly he wanted it. I left the fourth handful on the ground and stepped away. Salty came in and took up this final mouthful with a loud snort.

I do not make a habit of feeding wild animals in parks or anywhere else. On the other hand, we were far from any park and the deer was thirsty as well as hungry. There hadn't been rain for some time and I noticed the small bridges we crossed spanned dry streambeds. That explained Salty's desire for water. No doubt there were other water sources deep in the forest he could go to for a drink, but we were present and Salty had seemingly little fear of humans. Obviously there had been hikers, not thousands or hundreds maybe, but enough for Salty to trust us and take a chance. The deer hung around while we repacked the tent and sleeping bags and hoisted our backpacks to our shoulders. When we carried on down the trail Salty did not follow—he was grazing the grass at our campsite.

In the same way the deer found water and food in an unexpected way, we often find spiritual food and drink from God where we might not be looking for it—at a movie, in a conversation at the coffee shop, on a hike or hunt with a friend, talking with a stranger at a local sporting goods store. It happens in church and outside of church. Sometimes God's intervention may be a surprise and just the boost we needed. Sometimes it may even be a matter of life and death, physically and spiritually.

The trail that runs through our backyard and borders a trout stream brings all sorts of animals to our house. Mostly, it brings deer. In the fall, they eat leaves that have fallen from the cottonwoods and elm trees. In the summer and spring, they crop grass and flowers and plants. When winter arrives, they paw at the snow to get down to grass or leaves long fallen and long dead. Where leaves have been raked into piles at the back and left to molder, the deer will clear the snow and feed for weeks. If the snow is particularly deep, its crust hard, and the weather harsh, the deer are in trouble.

I had no idea how much trouble until I saw a doe and her fawn standing on our deck one winter. They were at the picnic table, where I had set out a platform for the birds and covered it with seeds. The doe was taking in the birdseed as fast as she could swallow. When the fawn leaned in and tried to get a mouthful the doe raised her front hoof and slammed it down on the table, forcing the fawn back. I was shocked. The doe must have been starving to deny food to her young.

What I wound up doing for the starving deer in my yard is not much different from what the Rocky Mountain Elk Foundation strives to do for elk or what Ducks Unlimited attempts to do for waterfowl. I knew I would not be able to stop the possibility of a massive crash in the deer population due to starvation, often brought about by too many deer and too few predators, but why could I not help the two or three dozen that made their way onto our property during a rough winter? Why couldn't I help the doe and her fawn the same way I put out birdseed to help the chickadees and sparrows and nuthatches? So I bought more seed, dug away the hard-crusted snow so the deer could reach the grass, and cleared away drifts to make piles of raked leaves easier to graze.

Isn't it true we need God to do for us what we try to do for elk and mallards and deer? There are times when we pant for water, we ache for real food, we feel like we are going to die inside if we don't get something strong for our souls. We need God to put out more seed, break up the snow and ice of our lives, clear away what blocks us from finding him and his words and his Spirit so that we can thrive. These are the times when we can't do it for ourselves—what we try isn't working and the things that are coming against us have pretty much knocked us flat and turned us inside out. We're losing it. We need God to intervene in an extraordinary way and bring special people and special circumstances into our situation to save us.

I have no idea how many deer we saved by our efforts. They were grateful for the extra seed and the clearing away of ice and snow that permitted them to feed on leaves and grass. They thronged the yard. Eventually the warm winds we call Chinooks melted back the ice, and the deer found plenty to eat. They were in and out of our yard and our neighbor's yard and grazing up and down the stream bank. Life for the deer, even that doe and fawn who had been famished earlier in the winter, was back to normal. I recognized them when they showed up at our place in the spring. They had their particular way about them, as all animals do, including wild ones. The fawn was bigger and fatter now, but still followed its mother in the same way and with the same gait. They nibbled in the front, at the side of the house, poked their noses around the picnic table, which was empty of seed, and settled in at the back to some serious feeding. The fawn had seen my son on a number of occasions putting out fresh seed, and I have to believe that was the reason for the peculiar thing that happened next!

Micah's bedroom was at the back of the house facing the creek. He always slept with his window wide open no matter what time of year it was. One morning he told me he kept hearing someone walking in the old autumn leaves under his window every night. When we took a good look we could see there was a place where an animal—or person—had bedded down. Micah was kind of spooked, but a day or two later I was able to solve the mystery for him.

I was out early before the sun was up, taking care of something or other, and happened to go to the backyard to look for a shovel. My steps were quiet on the spring grass and there were no old brown leaves on my path to crackle under my boots. When I rounded the house I found the winter fawn curled up under Micah's window. The mother was bedded down quite a ways off by a big cottonwood. The fawn did not lift its head—it was sound asleep, perfectly content to be as close as it could get to one of the persons who had given it food when it could not find food for itself.

Just a coincidence you might say? A fluke? Wild animals can be pretty smart and they have good memories—so maybe it was much more than that. In the same way we remember the God who helps us through tough times, maybe they remember the sons and daughters of God who, in his name, do the same thing for the other creatures God has made and also called good.

12

The Summer of the Gun

Therefore they shall be as the morning cloud and
as the early dew that passeth away, as the chaff
that is driven with the whirlwind out of the floor,
and as the smoke out of the chimney.

Hosea 13:3 KJV

They told me Jimmy Blacks killed two people and had spread
the word from his hiding place that he would kill more. There
was a list, and everyone on the list was going to die. I found
out one day my wife's name was written on Jimmy Blacks's
piece of paper.

Long before the shootings, I had practically pushed my wife
onto the plane north to get her to take a job as an outpost
nurse in a remote British Columbia community. The place
where her clinic was located only had a population of a dozen,
along with a country store, gas station, a library, and a town
hall. But the woods and mountains all around contained
thousands of people. Many of them had no running water or

power. Some had gas generators that enabled them to enjoy electricity, while others were content to cook on woodstoves and light candles or kerosene lamps at night. A year before we came, they were still using phones you had to crank to get an operator or to call a friend. It was raw, rugged, and beautiful backcountry where cowboys galloped through the streets with Winchesters strapped to their saddles on their way to the high pastures where livestock roamed.

Linda, as one of the two outpost nurses, had a Suburban 4x4 as well as a Ford Bronco to get around in. A helicopter pad across the street permitted medevac or dustoff choppers to land, pick her up, and race her to people in emergency situations—someone with a broken neck from a rollover on a gravel road, burn victims, men and women who had slashed themselves with axes or hatchets, people suffering from cardiac arrests.

When she was not on call, we hiked the magnificent country where families lived as if it were still the 1800s. Wolf packs ran free, and beef cattle grazed in mountain meadows frequented by cougar and grizzly. Back at the clinic, I helped with phones and paperwork and, on my own time, wrote and published my first book. We'd only been married four years. Yukon and Nahanni, our coyote-lab dogs, were scarcely a year old. And the nearest police or doctors were a three-hour drive east or west. It was a rough and tumble Old West Eden where the store had to stock hundreds of yards of lamp wick and gallons of kerosene as if it were 1875; women swore bear fat was better for baking a perfect biscuit than butter; and grizzlies, moose, coyote, wolves, and black bear could wander through town anytime they pleased as if they owned the place.

People made their way to the region, a plateau between the British Columbia interior and the Pacific Ocean, because it was the last frontier. Americans and Germans lived there, not just visited in an RV—they bought homes, cleared land, and settled in. They were joined by Brits and Aussies and Swiss, as well as Canadians from all across the country. Whites and Native Americans mixed at all levels of society: school, cattle work, church, rodeos. Linda spent a lot of time each week nursing at various reserves in the area as well as taking care of ranchers and people in towns along her route. The land of turquoise lakes, whitewater, steelhead, and salmon was an incredible melting pot of characters of all races and inclinations.

But it was an Eden with a streak of the Fall running hard and sharp right through it. Stock growers meetings could be wild and abusive affairs as people argued furiously over range boundaries and grazing rights. Even though the countryside was heaped to the heavens with mountains and blue skies, and had more than enough of God's beauty to satisfy most men and women, there were always those who turned to alcohol, drugs, and violence to find what they felt creation or God Almighty couldn't give them. So holes already in the heart combined with the holes of substance abuse and made people emptier and more hollow than before. Somehow that turned out to be Jimmy Blacks's life.

I never found out why he shot the husband and wife who were working cattle in the high meadows. When word came to me about other names that were on the list, I didn't know most of them. Those I did know, good people, made it hard for me to understand what they could have done to warrant a death sentence. But when my wife's name joined the mix, I knew it had to be because of the time he brought his wife to the clinic with severe injuries several months before.

It didn't take Linda and her partner Carol long to assess the damage and realize Jimmy Blacks had been beating his wife, Jackie. The clinic was attached to the living quarters of the staff members, so I happened to be readily available. Carol slipped out, asking me to stand by, so that she could call the police. I crouched by a door that opened right into the treatment room—if I heard fighting or scuffling I was to come flying in and take Jimmy down. Of course, the RCMP were hours away, but the nurses had a plan to delay the Blacks by insisting on further examinations, procedures, and treatments.

This worked for about half an hour. Coiled on the other side of the door, every muscle tensed, scarcely breathing, I strained to hear what was going on in the clinic—were voices raised in anger, was Jimmy threatening them, did someone just pick up a chair? Suddenly feet moved fast, the front door to the clinic swung open, and truck doors slammed. My wife poked her head out to say Jimmy's sixth sense had kicked in and he'd figured out what they were up to. I joined Linda and Carol at the clinic window as the pickup swerved off down the road, gravel popping under its tires. The two nurses shook their heads.

"Why can't you bring in the RCMP anyway?" I asked.

"She won't tell the truth about her injuries unless we can get her in a safe environment and away from him," my wife explained. "That's not going to happen while he's breathing down her neck. Especially now. He'll be suspicious."

Suspicious. And angry. Once he killed his first two, Jimmy Blacks decided he might as well go after everyone who had ever gotten on his wrong side. Two nurses who had tried to turn him in to the RCMP had definitely done that.

So it became the summer of people sleeping with loaded firearms under their beds, the summer of locked doors and locked windows and locked vehicles, the summer of looking over your shoulder—particularly if word came down that your name was on the piece of paper in the pocket of Jimmy's Storm Rider jacket.

When we came back from a road trip that summer, it looked to me like someone had tried to break into the clinic through the back door. The RCMP were in the neighborhood and took a look. Some of the damage was old, some might be fresh. What could they say? Maybe Jimmy, maybe not. Jimmy could be anywhere.

The police were trying to track him, but this was virgin wilderness. Planes had gone down in the mountains with gold on board and never been found. Roads were few. One gravel lane was the only way in or out by car or truck. The land around us was sometimes reached by boats crawling up inlets from the Pacific, but even then a party of men could only get so far after striking out from where they were moored. The forest was thick, unlogged, and impenetrable. The bears and wolves, fat on prey and carrion, were huge. Only wild animals had made roadways through the forests, and they weren't easy to follow. Jimmy Blacks could live on fish and rabbit and hide out in the woods and hills all summer. Ten thousand men with hounds might never catch a glimpse of him.

I kept a Marlin 45-70 in those days for protection from bears. It was a big-bore rifle that could fire as many as six or seven large bullets as fast as you worked the lever. The firearm was often used by trappers or guides in the bush to put down charging predators fast. It wasn't under my bed, but it was always near at hand. The hardest part for me was that Linda still had visits to make out on the road and I couldn't go along on all of them. Much as I wanted to be lord and protector, I could only do so much to keep her safe. Prayer became more than something to tag on at the end of church services or words to bless a meal with. I needed her to come home to me alive. It's funny, isn't it, that no matter how much you say you believe in God and Christ, you really reach out when danger lurks at the door of those you love and you're helpless to do much about it. You become a man of prayer because it is the best thing you can do.

The whole thing came to a head one afternoon in August. Linda arrived at one of her stops late—unusual for her, but a blessing for both of us. Road delays meant she got there after Jimmy Blacks had been discovered in the town, after his wife had fled from the house where he was holding her hostage, after the Emergency Response Team (ERT) squad was in place with helmets, Kevlar vests, and automatic weapons. She called me on her radiophone, and I asked her to be careful and to stay well away from the action.

We had no idea her radiophone was on the same frequency as those of the ERT force. As I told her I loved her and was praying for her, Linda saw the men look around at one another in confusion. Finally, the commander figured out it was the blond nurse and asked Linda not to use the phone while the operation was in progress. She told me that, despite the seriousness of the moment, a number of the heavily armed police were grinning at one another. We even brought up the matter of groceries in our chat.

Negotiations failed. Jimmy Blacks had no intention of coming out of the house and loosed a flurry of shots. On signal, tear gas canisters were fired through the windows. Crashing glass mixed with the thump of the explosives. Gas filled the home. The front door was knocked down and the first men charged in, firearms ready, masks on.

Jimmy was already dead. He'd shot himself rather than be taken prisoner. He had created a hideout in the sealed-off crawl space under the house and covered a trapdoor in the floor with a rug and a chair. When Jimmy hadn't been making his way through the woods, he was in the house or down in the hole. The chair and rug had been shoved to the side, the trapdoor hung open, and Jimmy was sprawled unmoving on the earth.

When Linda made it home and I ran out to hold her in my arms, it was not only to tell her I loved her and that I thanked God she was okay. It was also to hear her say how painful it had been to watch several people crying once the police moved in on Jimmy Blacks.

"You don't know how it was, Linda," one of the women sobbed. "Jimmy wasn't always this way. He used to be a good man. He used to treat Jackie right. I wish this wasn't happening. I wish none of this ever had to happen."

So in the midst of our gratitude that Linda and many others who had been threatened were safe and alive, we stood in the clinic parking lot and prayed for God to help Jackie recover, for God to come close to the loved ones of the couple Jimmy had killed, for Jimmy's friends and family who were devastated by the summer's terrible chain of events—and we prayed for God to have mercy on Jimmy Blacks's soul.

"Do you think that I like to see wicked people die? says the Sovereign Lord. Of course not! I want them to turn from their wicked ways and live" (Ezekiel 18:23 NLT).

13

Wildfire

When thou passest through the waters, I will be
with thee; and through the rivers, they shall not
overflow thee: when thou walkest through the fire,
thou shalt not be burned; neither shall the flame
kindle upon thee.

Isaiah 43:2 KJV

House fires and city fires are deadly enough. When a fire
breaks out in the wilderness, it is even more deadly, for there
are not enough fire fighters or resources immediately at hand
to put it out.

It was July. Linda was on the road with all her nursing gear.
I was at the outpost clinic working at my desk. Strong whiffs
of smoke began to come in through the screen on the window
and I popped my head out the door to investigate. A couple
of miles east, white smoke rose from the forest. I got on the
phone to a neighbor. She said calls had gone in and officials

explained it was a small blaze, easily controlled, and there was a ground crew already there to put it out.

"How did it start?" I asked. "There hasn't been any lightning."

"Oh, it was the same ground crew that's getting it under control," she laughed. "They were burning off tall brush in the ditches and it got away on them."

I went back to my desk and continued to work. But I felt restless. The smell of smoke in the air had not diminished, so after ten minutes I walked outside again. The smoke was thicker and rose higher, and now there was a water bomber buzzing the site. I phoned my neighbor a second time.

"It's moving closer to the town," I said. "That's what it looks like to me."

"Me too," she responded. "But they say it's not in the trees and between the bomber and ground crew they've just about got it contained. There are no alerts and no evacuation orders."

A half hour later the fire had moved hundreds of yards toward us, the smoke a dense mix of gray and white that was sky high. You could see trees bursting into flame. The bomber would disgorge its load of water, vanish to a nearby lake where it would scoop up thousands of gallons more, then hurry back for another low swoop over the blaze. I began to think about what I would throw in the truck to race west. I called my wife on the radiophone.

"Look, there's a fire," I told her. "They say they have it contained, but they don't. Sit tight where you are until I tell you it's okay."

"Well, I'm already on my way back and have a lot of things to do at the clinic," she replied. "I'll be another hour. They'll have it out by then, won't they?"

"I don't think so."

"I'll see how far I can get. If they stop me, I'll sit it out from there. What about you?"

"If it hits the edge of town, I'll grab the dogs and whatever else I think is important and head west."

I prayed, she prayed, and I went back outside. Now the smoke was black and boiling up out of the forest. There were two bombers diving at the flames. As I watched, a third joined them. From its belly blasted a red wave of fire retardant. This time my neighbor called me.

"They're still saying it's under control," she let me know.

"Where are they calling from?" I asked. "Miami? Another hour and it'll be hitting the first ranch buildings."

"I know. Ben's got the pickup loaded."

I went back outside. Now I counted five or six bombers going at the blaze. Clearly someone was panicking now. I called my wife but could not reach her. I began to pile items in the truck, worry gnawing at the back of my mind. If I'd known what was going on with her at that moment I'd have been a lot more worried and praying a lot harder.

Linda was approaching the thick smoke of the fire and slowing down. There were men working at the edges of the blaze and trucks parked on both sides of the road. A man appeared out of the haze with a mask over his face and waved her down. He said the fire was contained near the roadway and fire fighting had moved farther into the forest. When he found out she was a nurse heading to her clinic, I suppose he decided she came under the category of emergency personnel.

"Go ahead," he told her. "Just be careful."

She had to be careful all right. He had no business waving her ahead into a fire zone, nurse or no nurse. It was one of the most frightening drives of her life. Flames were shooting up thousands of feet in streaks of yellow and red. Pine trees were disintegrating before her eyes—tall and green one moment, black skeletons wrapped in flame the next. Some crashed onto the roadway, causing her to swerve violently to avoid the burning wood and sparks. Ash covered her windshield, and scorched pinecones banged onto the roof and hood of the Suburban.

Linda fought an impulse to drive fast, even though she wanted to be through the fire as swiftly as possible. Smoke made visibility poor and the last thing she needed was an accident where no one on earth could help her. Praying, fighting down her fears, steering through a gloom lit again and again by explosions of flame, she made her way along the road. It seemed to her as if she were driving through hell. Even with her windows tightly shut she could hear the roar of the forest fire. It sounded like the howl of hurricanes that crawled up the eastern seaboard and blasted her home province of Nova Scotia.

We often look at verses or passages in the Bible and think they sound strong and inspiring. Rather than believe we will literally walk through fire unscathed, we temper a promise like that found in Isaiah 43:2 to mean we will get through the fires and troubles of life with God's help. But sometimes God expects us to take verses like that exactly as we find them—no, you will not be burned by real flames; no, you will not be physically set ablaze. In fact, that very verse was a key part of a book I was writing, and a promise the main character clung to throughout all his trials and tribulations.

But I was still surprised, when Linda made it home, that God would bring my wife safely through an actual inferno, not a symbolic one, preventing red hot coals from striking and blowing her tires, tangles of flame and branches from falling and blocking her path, and blackened trees from crushing the roof or engine block of her 4x4. It was amazing because the odds were that something nasty not only could, but would happen to a person driving through the middle of a fire storm. When I saw her vehicle emerge from the rolls of smoke, my feelings were a mix of surprise, relief, and anger—surprise that she had driven into a fireball, relief that God had brought her through unharmed, and anger that one of the ground crew had waved her forward into danger. But with her in my arms, relief and gratitude won out.

The water bombers and the men on the ground kept on fighting and bravely put an end to the fire. People unloaded their pickups and went back to their daily routines. I went back to writing my book and walking our dogs, Linda worked up her reports and took care of the injured who streamed into the clinic—anything from sawdust in the eye to thumbs or fingers partially severed while chopping kindling.

But every time we drove in and out of town heading east for the next couple of months, the blackened grass on both sides of the gravel road and the scorched tree trunks reminded us of what might have been and what, in fact, had been—a fire stopped, a community saved, and a young wife shielded from death and injury. The dark scene was a bright scene for us that spoke of God's mercy, his gift of life, and the words of Scripture that are real promises to his people.

14

White Death

Lord, remind me how brief my time on earth will be. Remind me that my days are numbered—how fleeting my life is.

Psalm 39:4 NLT

Death is more of a surprise in the wilderness. In our cities and towns, we are ready for dangers that may come our way—whether by traffic accidents, criminals, or hazards on the job. But when we go to the wilderness to relax and unwind, though we know there are things to guard against, death is not what we expect to face.

Fast and strong rivers are one of the great glories of the wilderness. Pristine and unpolluted, they are the hallowed grounds of fly-fishermen, kayakers, canoeists, and adventurers of all kinds. Fed by rains, underground springs, snowmelt, and glaciers, they race down mountain slopes and through forests and drop over high rock to form waterfalls and plumes of silver spray. Just to gaze at them is an inspiration. They are the bloodstream of the wilderness. Without them the forests, animals, birds, and fish would vanish and the land would become barren, practically lifeless.

I had done whitewater rafting with youth groups. I even baptized a teenager who insisted she be immersed in the sharp waters of a wilderness river—if I had let go of her, even for an instant, she would have been swept to her death. I had stepped from stone to stone along the quieter sections of such streams, my infant son in my arms, so he could hear and feel the language of the waters and the wild. I found spiritual strength in the fast rivers because God put heart in me by means of their power and hard beauty. I grew so aware of them, and was so used to people taking precautions when they ventured on or near them, that I never thought I would see death seize upon the rivers as a means of bringing people to their end.

Linda and I were heading out for the day, dogs in the back of the truck, outpost clinic in the capable hands of her nursing partner. Gassing up at the local pump, we talked with the owner about the whitewater that slashed through the woods all around us. He said the outfits that took people on the rivers had good reputations and had never lost anyone.

"Have you done whitewater?" he asked us.

"Well, not around here," I replied.

"Oh, you've got to. I highly recommend it. Nothing to worry about. You'd be as safe in one of their boats as you would standing on dry ground."

In retrospect, as soon as fifteen minutes later, his words would become tragically ironic.

We were driving along the gravel track that wound through the plateau, laughing and looking forward to a swim in a lake the color of a turquoise New Mexican stone, when a white RCMP truck came barreling toward us. Its lights were flashing, its siren blaring, and it was right in the middle of the road, leaving no room for anything or anyone else. The driver leaned on the horn and waved us out of the way with a glare of savage fury. I almost steered into the ditch to clear a path.

"What is going on?" I demanded, as if my wife should know.

"It's obviously a serious accident."

"But we didn't pass anything."

"It could be down one of the side roads."

It was down one of the side roads all right. And soon, both nurses knew the whole story even as bodies were being laid out on the riverbank. A group of American executives, one of them the vice president of a prestigious U.S. corporation, had been getting some serious rest and relaxation in the Canadian wilderness. It was one of the few ways they could totally relax and get away from the enormous stress of their work. But the waters were running high along the Class V river that spring, and markers along their route were not obvious to the guide because many were covered in water—boulders, deadheads, rocky cutbanks. Suddenly they were catapulted into the rough and relentless boil of whitewater. Suddenly five of them were dead.

The shock of dealing with violent death like this was reflected in the words of one of the police officers on the scene, the one who had almost run us off the road in his haste. He leaned on the hood of his truck one afternoon after the incident and shook his head: "I'm still not over that. I'm still not over that." This was a year later.

Yet the river was not finished taking the lives of men that spring. Although as an outpost nurse Linda received a good deal of information about the drownings, I still wasn't satisfied with what we'd been told about how it had happened. I watched the local news that night, where the tragedy was the main story. The TV station had managed to latch onto a German who was going to run the same river the very next day. Dressed in a wetsuit for his interview, speaking excellent English, he expressed his condolences to the families who had lost their loved ones, but then pointed out that the executives had not been properly prepared for whitewater rafting—had any of them worn helmets or wetsuits or gloves? A Class V was not a pleasure cruise; it was a true test of a person's whitewater skills and courage. You had to be fully alert and fully geared up. He did not have any concerns for his trip on the same stretch of water the next day because he was focused and equipped.

"I will be all right," he promised the reporter. "I will do it in the manner in which it should be done."

The next afternoon he was dead. Drowned in the same Class V river, killed by the same swirl of white foam, laid out on the same riverbank by the same police.

Further expeditions on the river were suspended pending an investigation.

Six people killed on North American highways over the span of two days is considered significant only to the families affected. Otherwise the number of fatalities is too small to draw much attention. In the wilderness, it is different: One or two hikers or hunters or whitewater rafters killed is a tragedy; five or six killed is a catastrophe and the media snags onto the story. It is one thing to die on the highways, where so many do. It is another to die in the splendor of nature and God's creation, where there is so much beauty and grace. Yet along with the beauty and grace there is still, underneath, a hard and unyielding edge.

"God has to nearly kill us sometimes," John Muir said, "to teach us lessons."[2]

2. Linnie Marsh Wolfe, *Son of the Wilderness: The Life of John Muir* (Madison, WI: University of Wisconsin Press, 1945, 1973, 2003), 105.

If we will not learn from our everyday life in the towns and cities of America and Canada of the transient quality of life, we who go into the great parks and wilderness spaces will learn it there. Most people have no idea when the end will come. There will be no warning for 90 percent of us and absolutely no sense of impending doom. Nor can we spend our lives worrying about it or we will die anyway after never having lived. What we can do is be ready at any time to go, and that is a tough thing for men and women to come to grips with.

We boast about ruling our destinies and teach this to our children as if it were some sort of God-given precept. But we are not the gods some say we are, nor are we the masters of our fate. Yes, there is much we can do to improve our lives and the lives of those around us. There are challenges to be met and overcome, things we ought to try to excel at, and these are concepts we should share with others and with our children.

But the wild places also teach us that while the mountains and forests and streams may endure thousands of years, man does not. Man is but a breath, a wildflower on a mountain slope, a hawk that circles his world for threescore and ten years—perhaps a bit more, perhaps much less (Psalm 90:10)—and then is gone from the earth to the place that God appoints. We are spirits and we leave our bodies behind until the new heaven and the new earth.

The hard question is this: Do we go in Christ to the One who made the wild places we find so much strength in, or do we ignore the Creator of heaven and earth and consider the wilderness a random act in a universe that came about by chance? Do we embrace the Maker of mountains and stars and elk and steelhead, and go where they may be found again in absolute perfection, or do we turn our back on such power, imagination, and love, and step into a reality devoid of beauty and magnificence?

"For we know that if the earthly tent which is our house is torn down, we have a building from God, a house not made with hands, eternal in the heavens" (2 Corinthians 5:1 NASB).

15

Fighting Bull

All the animals of the wilderness are mine, and
the cattle that are on the hills, and the bulls.

Psalm 50:10 Aramaic Bible in Plain English

There is a lot to learn about working cattle, especially if
you've never done it before. Not just cowboy lessons, but
life lessons.

The ranches scattered throughout the region where my
wife had her outpost clinic were of varying sizes, from a
few hundred acres to a few thousand. The injuries were all
fairly common—kicked by a horse, thrown from a horse,
foot or hand cut chopping wood, arm or leg ripped open on
barbed wire. Since Linda and I both rode, it made us highly
desirable as extra hands when livestock had to be moved
from one pasture to another or brought in for spring or fall
roundup. However, it's one thing to ride and another thing
to cowboy up.

Bill and Kate Tucker ran a six-thousand-acre spread. The stories I'd already heard coming out of the ranch were incredible.

A few ranchers said there'd been UFOs.

A trapper told me he'd been hired to kill a monster grizzly that kept frightening hundreds of cattle in summer pasture as it picked off one cow after another.

A cowboy swore Bill Tucker had a real honest to goodness old time chuck wagon he drove out onto the range when his hands were branding.

Having grown up in the '60s and '70s with holsters and cap guns—watching TV shows like *Rawhide, Wanted: Dead or Alive, Gunsmoke, Have Gun—Will Travel, Bonanza,* and *The High Chaparral,* shows that had forged a code and ethic in a generation—I jumped at the chance to help Bill Tucker move cattle on his ranch . . . and made Linda jump too.

There are ranches bigger than six thousand acres in North America, but it was the largest one I'd ever been on, cut through with rivers and streams and strewn with forests of ponderosa pine. Like many ranchers, the Tuckers also had grazing rights on federal or crown land that made riding their spread a larger-than-life experience. Deer were in the woods, of course, but so were elk and timber wolf, and overhead you could spot golden eagles. With a Stetson on my head and a good quarter horse under me, I really did feel like I was in one of those westerns I'd enjoyed so much as a city boy.

It was a warm summer evening and the sun lingered a long time in the sky, as it always does at that time of year in the high latitudes—it wouldn't set until 10:00 or 10:30 at night. Tucker had six or seven of us, including his wife and daughter, to move a couple of hundred head up to greener pastures. The herd was a mix of steers, cows, and a bull. The bull was dehorned, so even though he was a good size, I didn't think he'd be any trouble, even after Kate Tucker expressed misgivings about moving him at the same time as the others.

"Why, do you expect trouble?" I asked.

She shook her head. "Not really. But calling someone bull-headed has its start with critters like this here, so there's no telling what might happen with Smokey."

Linda and I watched like hawks and quickly learned how to bring strays back into the herd and to block others from attempting to leave the main group. I found it satisfying to trail a cluster of breakaway cows and heifers and push them to where Linda had planted her horse firmly in their path, with a ridge to the side, so that seeing her, the cattle had no choice but to bawl their protests and return to the herd. We did this a number of times and became something of a team. Sometimes we'd each ride out on our own to bring in a threesome. I felt solid in the saddle and my wife looked just as comfortable. It was a pleasure to see her, back straight, boots in the stirrups, blond hair streaming out behind her as she galloped.

The drive was something of a dream ride until the bull decided he didn't want to keep going. He began to stand still, like a big black rock. When he was prodded he would start up again, but stop a few minutes later. Then he began to swing his head and turned back in the direction we'd just come from. Before anyone could move against him, he'd broken into a trot, shoving his way through the cows and steers, panicking some, and getting others to head back as well. Suddenly we had a bawling, whirling mass of confusion on our hands.

"He'll turn the whole herd!" exclaimed Kate. "Stop him, Murray!"

Why she called upon me I have no idea. I suppose one reason was that her husband was too far ahead to get involved. There were few riders near us to give a hand and, I suppose, that was another. She'd already figured out I was not quite as green as good grazing grass, so I figure that was a third. Whatever her reasons, it was a command I was not about to ignore. I pounded after Smokey and put myself, and my horse Tempest, in front of him.

The bull dodged. The horse had been trained to work with cattle, anticipated his move, and got in front again. For a moment the bull seemed to consider going the way we wanted him to go. Then came the head swing, a roar, and he almost ran over a steer to get around us to the left. We galloped ahead and cut him off a third time.

Now Smokey had had enough. Down went his head. I swung Tempest and we danced out of the way as he lunged. His mind was no longer focused on coming or going, but on getting us—he charged, missed, bellowed, and charged again. Each time we skipped aside and moved to block him from heading farther from the herd. Each time he only cared about lowering his head and going furiously for the horse's flank.

After four or five of these attacks, even a greenhorn like me realized it was only a matter of time before my horse stumbled or misstepped. Or the bull plowed into a cow. Or broke his neck against a tree. I backed off and let him hurl himself at thin air until he could see that no one was stopping him from going where he wanted to go. Smokey glanced about, spotted us a good many yards away, and fixed us with a glare. Then he headed right back to where we had started the herd hours before.

I didn't know what to do next—should I lasso him and hope I did a better job than a city slicker? While I thought hard and watched him stride insolently toward his destination, Kate Tucker came up beside me on her horse.

"That's fine," she said, as if she could read my thoughts. "You did the right thing by letting him have his way. An angry bull is a big problem for everyone and if he slammed his weight into Tempest, you'd wind up with a dead or injured horse. If the rider ends up on the ground the bull could go after him too."

She smiled. "You sure thought quick enough for someone new to the business. We might just make a top-dollar hand out of you yet!"

Part of me had wanted to keep at the bull until I got what I wanted, making me just as bullheaded as he was. That part could have gotten the bull or Tempest killed. Even I could have wound up on a gurney. In the end, the bull made his way back to his old fenced-in pasture and was content, while the rest of the herd carried on to new grass. We were finished well before sunset and walked our horses back to the main ranch for a home-cooked beef dinner.

In the spiritual life, just as in the physical life, you have to know when to keep at something and when enough is enough. It's not easy to figure out because no one wants to quit just because the going is tough. Jesus knew when it was time to leave a town that didn't want him around or didn't have the faith needed to help bring miracles to reality. After he set the possessed man in the graveyard free, the citizens of the place begged him to get out and he did. He told his followers there were times to shake the dust from their feet and move on to the next town.

On the other hand, Jesus saw his mission through to the end. He could have quit in Gethsemane but chose to do the right thing instead—what his Father wanted. Peter was encouraged to pick up the pieces after betraying Jesus and get back to a life of spiritual commitment. Paul learned to stick with the things God brought into his life and disregard the things that took him away from what mattered most—faith, hope, and love.

These are the important decisions we have to make as we go, and we need our friends, our church, our times of prayer, and God's words to help us. Whether we face down bulls or back off is up to us to figure out, with Christ at our side. Jesus told us never to stop praying about what things to leave alone and what things to go after with all our hearts (Luke 18:1–8).

16

Shootout!

I am for peace, but when I speak, they are for war!

Psalm 120:7 ESV

Sometimes a man goes into the wild to be alone, completely alone, and sometimes that aloneness is for a long time. But when hard times befall us, being alone, as much as you may have sought it, can be a little too difficult to bear.

Ernst lived in a valley far south of the outpost clinic. Purple mountains rimmed the horizon and purple sage rolled over the fields. The sky was seemingly infinite in its scope. His horses had plenty of hay, the stove in his log cabin had plenty of wood, and Ernst had plenty of clean air to take in by the lungful.

"Europe is too crowded," he told us. "Do you know how cramped it was for me living in Zurich? Now I can hear streams running and birds calling. At night it is starlight not streetlights. The silence itself has a sound. This is what Switzerland looked like a thousand years ago. I am content."

He had a small remuda, or herd of horses, he used for riding and ranching. They were spirited steeds he could not exercise adequately on his own. So he welcomed riders who knew what they were doing and who would not abuse his mares and geldings. He asked us to give the two mounts he picked out a good run on a flat meadow not far from the cabin.

"Open the gate in the fence and you will find the field," he explained. "Stay out as long as you wish, but please spare some time for a cup of tea with me afterward."

It was big country and we rode over a great deal of it, including the meadow that had no gopher holes, where Linda and I galloped and raced and shouted at each other. The sun was bright as fire with a summer's edge to it, keen as a well-sharpened Bowie knife. The scent of sage and clover and sweet hay was thick on our jeans and denim jackets when we finally brought the horses back to Ernst's corral. As promised, tea was brewed and waiting for us and we sat with him inside his small living room of log furniture and heavy cotton throws. Inside such a handcrafted space, or outside in God's handcrafted one, I find it easy to worship and easy to believe. Sometimes the things that hone a man's spirit are harder to find in the knots and twists of cities and asphalt streets.

We chatted a long time. Thinking this man who had chosen solitude had had enough, Linda and I got up to leave. He seemed reluctant to let us go.

"I like my quiet and peace," he explained. "But sometimes, I confess, it can get a little too quiet and a little too peaceful. I did not always feel this way. But sit back down, have some more tea, and let me tell you about a friend. It is losing him that has made the land too big and too lonely for me now."

His friend, an American, had come to the high, wide, and lonely plateau with its raw forests, fast rivers, and sawtooth peaks just as he had, from a foreign land and with a longing for as much space and freedom as possible. Like Ernst, Jack had purchased acreage and cut a small ranch out of the wilderness, built a cabin with his own logs, nurtured a meadow as a hayfield, and brought five or six good horses into his corral.

Neighbors—which meant they were ten miles apart—Jack and Ernst rode together, hunted, fished, and made furniture to use or sell together, and when the winter nights got too long, shared fire, and food, and sharp-starred skies as well. Even when the American fell in love and married a local beauty whose father and mother had a spread a hundred miles away, she (Bets) insisted Ernst remain a part of their lives, and he did. Once a month the three of them got together at one cabin or the other for a long meal, a long conversation, an overnight, and a full breakfast cooked over the woodstove in the morning. Ernst had the solitude he craved. And he had the human companionship he needed when weeks of silence turned into months of too much silence. But trouble was brewing.

Men can bring goodness and strength into the wilderness or they can bring bitterness and violence. God permits either in a scarred wild that has equal measures of goodness and violence of its own among its wolves and deer and cougar. An old man who had a place in the hills even deeper into the wilds had years before taken a liking to the pretty ranch girl Bets and sought to woo her, even though there was more than fifty years between them. Bets had been kind to him while trying to let him know she was not the sort of woman he should be marrying. This was unfortunately a mistake which only stoked his ardor. He felt she was playing a young woman's game and that he simply needed to persist with gifts of flowers and cards to win her hand.

When the American came into the picture, the old man flew into a rage and warned Jack off. Bets was *his* woman and he'd fight to keep it that way if the Yank went too far. Bets tried to calm him down and create the same sort of three-way friendship she had with Ernst, but the old man was having none of it. It was him she loved, not Jack, and he'd do whatever necessary to ensure their relationship was not endangered. No man, no matter who he was or where he came from or how tall he stood in his riding boots, was going to jeopardize that.

Finally, Bets stopped receiving the old man's letters and gifts and refused to speak with him anymore. She and Jack were engaged and then married, Ernst standing up for his friend. Bets moved into the log cabin with her American husband and put daisies in jars of water on the rough kitchen table and hung wreaths of purple sage on the front door.

The old man went wild with jealousy. He let it be known that no man or woman could treat him the way they had and he would square matters with the two of them before the summer was out. Making the trip down to the big city in his '58 Jimmy, he withdrew all the cash from his account, bought some new firearms and plenty of ammo, and headed back into the hills, muttering threats, not caring who heard them.

People warned Jack and Bets, and the couple took precautions. Jack had built a one-room cabin with a bed that served as a couch in the daytime. He and Bets each kept loaded guns at their bedside tables—underneath the bed might not offer fast enough access if trouble came. When they went about their business on the ranch, they had guns with them at all times. Maybe the old coot wouldn't try anything at all, Jack confided to Ernst, but then again, he just might lose it, come completely unglued, and try to blow their heads off. So Bets and Jack lived their lives like people on the western frontier had a hundred years before, regularly glancing over their shoulders, worrying about bandits or war parties swooping down on them at a moment's notice.

The old man roared into the cabin early one morning while they were still in bed. He kicked in the front door with guns literally blazing. Jack and Bets grabbed their firearms and fired back at him as rapidly as they could. Police found bullet holes in the walls, the ceiling, the floor, the doorframe, the windowsills, and the fence posts outside. Windowpanes were blown out and blood spattered the log furniture, the floorboards, and the quilt bedspread.

Bullets ripped through the cabin and into the yard as the three fired back and forth. The horses must have kicked up a tremendous fuss in the corral. Finally, the attacker sank to the floor, riddled with bullets, bleeding out. Bets and Jack, shot to pieces, died in the bed in each other's arms. Ernst was too far away to hear the gunfire and never knew what had happened until after the RCMP had been called to the scene and discovered the bodies. The news hit him like a fist to the stomach.

"Now and then, you know, the loneliness of living out here gets to me again," Ernst said to us, his eyes dark. "I actually think about driving over to see Jack, just for a split second. Then I remember he is dead and I cannot visit him, not ever. So my sense of loneliness increases. I go for a long ride and I might see some deer or elk, perhaps get a glimpse of a wolf near sunset. I take in the stars, the moon making the snow on the mountains shine like glass, and after a while I am all right again and glad I am living here in the forests and hills. But it may take days for me to turn around."

We prayed with Ernst before we left, talked about his love for what God had made and how much that same God loved him. But there was no getting around the fact that for some the wild places are a tonic while for others they are a poison.

Isolation brings one man peace and another is twisted by it. There are those in the wilderness who find Christ and recover what was missing, while others find the devil and lose the best part of who they were.

The wilderness can be a sanctuary for some and a pit for others. It depends what you bring to it and what you take out of it. How much better if a man can be still in the quiet magnificence of the peaks and valleys and, above anything else, know there is a God—a God of powerful love who can put that same powerful love in their own hearts and change them from the inside out, healing all maladies of the human spirit.

17

Lost

A righteous man cares for the needs of his animal.
Proverbs 12:10 NIV 1984

A man may well go farther for his wife, children, and friends, but he will also go far to save the life of a favorite dog or horse.

Yukon and Nahanni were about one year old when we arrived in the wilderness surrounding the outpost clinic. They had actually been born in a household that soon after experienced the bitter pangs of separation and divorce. For reasons I never understood, the mother dog and her pups wound up in a monastery for several weeks. Their next stop was supposed to be an animal shelter, but somehow our landlords managed to get their hands on the four and kept them at the house where we rented a basement suite. In the end, they adopted the mother and her black puppy, while we took in the other puppies, whom we eventually named Yukon and Nahanni.

They were great companions right from the beginning, and once the children were born they became great guard dogs. Smart, fast, obedient, loyal, and brave, they would obviously make terrific hunting dogs as well. But long before the children, and long before they were old enough to hunt, we lost the dogs to the wild for a time.

Since they had been born and raised in Vancouver, the brother and sister puppies had never seen snow. When they were eighteen months old, we took them on a January walk so they could sniff around among the vast pines and rocky outcrops beyond the outpost clinic's yard. They always dogged our heels, so we removed their leashes and let them roll about, burrow their noses in the white stuff, and generally have a good time. While this was going on, Linda and I were briefly distracted by the sight of a stag high up on a ridge within our plain view. When we turned back around, Yukon and Nahanni were gone.

The northern wild had proven to be a stronger draw than my wife or I had imagined. We quickly followed their paw prints into the woods. It took fifteen minutes of hunting and calling to find Nahanni, and by then we were worried and upset. Nahnani got a tongue-lashing and Linda snapped the leash back on her collar. Together we followed prints that ran straight for the heart of the forest, shouting Yukon's name. He never came to us. After several hours we went back to the clinic for food and drink. We had no intention of giving up the search, but we needed to replenish ourselves. And Linda had to work that afternoon and take care of walk-ins.

I was hoping Yukon would follow our tracks back to the clinic. When he didn't show up, I went out again and spent another two hours tramping about among the trees without any luck, shouting myself hoarse. Often I stood still and simply listened. The forests sprawled west for hundreds and hundreds of miles and human habitations were few. I could only hear the breeze moving cautiously among the limbs of the evergreens—no sounds of men's voices or the chopping of wood or the bark of a dog. Late in the afternoon I returned to the clinic again. Discouraged, I slumped in my chair with my parka on while my wife tried to lift my spirits.

I had always wanted a dog. As a boy I'd had a cocker spaniel for a short time before my parents gave it away. Yukon and Nahanni had dropped out of the sky into our lives, and I had quickly bonded with the pair. It was like being a boy all over again and the world suddenly seemed so very young when we went to the seashore and parks together—they ran, they fought, they swam, chased sticks. Now the prospect of losing the male when we'd had barely more than a year together, instead of twelve or fifteen, hit me harder than I'd expected. We had only looked at the stag for seconds—just seconds—how could Yukon vanish completely in that short space of time?

I walked back into the woods a third time. I was under no illusions. Cougar, coyote, and wolf were under the dark pines. Up by the landing strip where bush planes came in, timber wolves regularly left their mark. Hunting in a pack, they made a wide trail with paw impressions that staggered me by their size—surely these were small bears, not wolves? Of course, bears didn't travel that way and the tracks were definitely canine, but the circumference of the prints made me go to a local, long-time trapper and ask if I was somehow mistaken. He shook his head when I met him at the log cabin restaurant.

"The timber wolves around here are over one hundred pounds apiece, closer to one fifty, never mind what the textbooks tell you about them being in the eighties," he rumbled. "How tall are you? Six? Six four? They'll come to your hip

or more. Those are their prints, son. Big beasts. Especially
the blacks."

Yukon, an eighteen month old, wouldn't be able to fend off
a coyote attack, let alone the charge of a timber wolf pack. I
walked and called, plunging deeper into the forest than I had
with Linda and Nahanni, deeper than I had since our arrival
at the small town in the British Columbia interior. I found a
dead muskrat, far from any pond or marsh, curled up at the
base of a tree, in perfect condition, not a mark on its body,
not a ruffle in its fur, not a drop of blood on the snow, but
still stone frozen dead. I looked at it and thought of Yukon
curled up and dead in the same way, his bones eventually
becoming part of the great northern wilderness, and it made
my heart sick. Couldn't we have had a life together? What
was the harm in that?

Of course, I prayed. Why wouldn't I? Would any man let
his best saddle horse go easily if it were lost in the same way?
Would he let his best hunting dog, or any one of his dogs,
vanish without some sort of effort to track him down and
rescue him? I asked God to let me enjoy being a boy again
with Yukon, to have a life together I'd never had with any
dog or any animal. I asked him if he hadn't had a dog when
he was a boy in Israel, if he hadn't meant for them to become
one of man's greatest friends and bravest protectors—if he
hadn't planned that I myself should have one or two close
by my side for a decade or more. Wouldn't Yukon and Nahanni's companionship make a difference in my life, along
with a wife and children and work for my hands and heart?

God answers some prayers the way we hope and others
not. Some of the sick are healed and recover and others go
back to him. Some of the knots in our lives and our children's
lives are untangled right away and others take years, even a
lifetime. He is God—he loves us, but he is free to do what

he thinks is right, even if we can't even begin to understand his reasons. When you pray, you have to accept those terms.

Hours before a hard death, Jesus asked if the cup could be set aside, if something else could be done to redeem the human race, anything else, rather than his having to drain the cup and become sin so that we could get a chance at real life and become the righteousness of God (2 Corinthians 5:21). But the Father said no, this was how it had to be. Jesus accepted that. And died.

So anything was possible, anything could happen. God knew what I wanted. He also knew that I acknowledged his rule and that his will was absolute, and I wanted it to be absolute, in heaven and on earth. So I walked farther and farther until I did not know where to walk anymore. I stopped at a particular place, surrounded by ponderosa pine, and said I would go no farther. I had to return to my wife and our home—the sun was setting. I prayed a final prayer and waited. Nothing. Long miles into the wilderness now, I knew it was time to retrace my steps.

Then it happened. As if it were a movie with a classic happy ending. Not *Old Yeller* or *Marley and Me*. More like *The Incredible Journey* and *Homeward Bound,* where the dogs and cat make it. I heard the swishing of snow in a forest where I had heard nothing but wind in the branches all day. I heard the unmistakable sound of paws hitting the ground. I turned in complete shock to see a white body hurtling up the track of my boot prints like a rocket. I dropped to my knee and Yukon threw himself into me, whining and yipping and licking my face without stopping.

I was never more stunned in my entire life. I drew that happy animal against my chest and hugged him and laughed—I couldn't believe it. It felt like the scene was happening in my imagination. That I was daydreaming about how good it could be if God said yes. But the oversized puppy paws were real, along with the white fur and the ears that had just come up tall and sharp. It was Yuke, as I often called him, the Yuke I wanted a life with, the life and friendship I had asked God for.

And we got it. Yukon lived to be fifteen and the adventures and experiences of his lifetime cram my heart and soul to this day. It's impossible to think of not having had those years with him—what a different and poorer life mine would have been. But God knew we needed each other and he made it happen. Even though the loss, when it eventually came, was almost too much to bear, I thank God I had those years despite the pain that came at their end.

If it is true that a righteous man, a good man, cares for his animals, as the Bible says, I think it is also true that a good animal cares for his master. That, at least, has been my experience with two sets of canine brothers and sisters—all four of them loved me, my wife, and my children with all the love God put in their animal kingdom hearts.

When we reached home that night, Linda grinned, hugged, and kissed us in her delight, then I lay down on the couch to sleep, exhausted physically and emotionally, and Yukon lay right beside me on the carpet. Nahanni was near at hand, never wanting to let the two of us out of her sight again. For a time, while we were still awake, Yukon kept putting his paw up to my chest, and I eventually held it in my hand to let him know I was there and not going anywhere. Finally, hanging on to each other just like that, we slept, and did not wake until the strong and bright mountain dawn.

18

A Horse for Christmas

I have compared thee, O my love, to a company
of horses in Pharaoh's chariots.

Song of Solomon 1:9 KJV

In the wilderness it is especially clear that Christmas is not about things, but about family, friends, and faith.

Christmastime was white and sparkling at the outpost clinic, unlike the green and wet Christmases of Vancouver, which had been our experience for several years before heading north. I took the truck to a lonely stretch of forest, let the dogs pile out and chase each other through the snow, and cut down a lodgepole pine with a steel bucksaw. Unfortunately, it looked better in the forest than it did in our small living room. Without all the other pines around it, our tree appeared thin and scraggly. On the other hand, it was real and it filled the house with the powerful scent of evergreen and the Canadian north. We decorated it simply and placed our presents underneath, including the dogs' rawhide bones, which they always managed to sniff out.

Of the dozen or so people who lived right by the clinic, the youngest were Mack and Megan. We'd shared meals together, and Mack, a ranch hand, always made me laugh when he ate my "old recipe" chuck wagon stew. The stew had whole onions in it, big as apples, and Mack would ladle these into his bowl, carve them up with knife and fork, and gobble them down.

"They're meant to add flavor to the stew," I told him. "You're supposed to leave them in the pot."

Mack grunted. "If they're in the pot then they're part of the stew. And if they're part of the stew they're meant for eating."

Eating at their log home, we would sit talking until the room grew dark, at which point Mack or Megan lit candles and oil lamps so we could see one another's faces—no candles burned for effect at their place (unlike our home). Nor was the wood crackling in the fireplace for effect either. It was there to keep us warm, not to make us feel romantic.

So when Mack came by on his horse, just before noon on Christmas Day, I knew that riding the few hundred yards when he could have walked wasn't for effect either. He swung down, gave us Christmas greetings, and extended the horse's reins to me.

"I know you both like to ride and you got no horses of your own. So take Charlotte out. That's my merry Christmas gift to the two of you."

Linda was pretty excited so I invited her to go first. Mack adjusted the stirrups and Linda began to walk Charlotte up the road that wound around the hill in back of the clinic. The mare was milk white with a long mane. Linda was blond and her blue eyes were flashing. Horse and rider suited each other. It was so mild and sunny, in the 40s, that my wife wore no hat. Her hair fell loosely down her back as Charlotte vanished in the trees high above us, Linda smiling and holding the reins lightly.

I made Mack coffee as black as night—I had no stew onions handy—and we sat down to talk about wolves he'd photographed, beef cattle, what January weather was going to be like, and whether he'd take Megan for a drive to the coast for New Year's Eve—such a drive was simply a matter of carrying straight on west along the gravel highway until snow became rain, pine trees became cedars, and ocean waves replaced frozen lakes. There was no lack of subjects to talk about. He even wanted to know about my writing. One hour became two, two started heading on toward three. Both of us got restless at the same time.

"Lin should have been back by now," I said, worrying. "I know she's good with a horse, but she's never been alone in the hills—there's a lot out there that could spook a horse and throw a rider."

"Char's steady," Mack encouraged me. "Still, it's been a while. We should probably take a look."

We climbed in my truck and headed up the road Lin had used. The airstrip was up there, the rodeo grounds, hayfields covered in snow, and hundreds of miles of forest backed by sharp white peaks. Every now and then I stopped, and Mack got out to check for fresh hoofprints. Lin had left the road after about a mile and headed into the woods. Mack would ask me to slow down and he'd point to where she had emerged from the forest, cantered a short distance in the open, and returned to the trees. She did this several times.

For half an hour we looked and finally parked by a meadow. We knew she was alive and still on horseback and were certain she would come out into the field at some point to run the mare. In the end, she surprised us by riding through a thick cluster of evergreens right by the truck and landing practically on top of us. She was so happy, so radiant, a smile opening up the beauty of her face, that neither Mack nor I could bring ourselves to chastise her. When we got out and stood by her and Charlotte, Linda reached down and patted the mare's neck.

"Was I gone long?" she asked. "It wasn't much more than an hour or two, was it?"

Mack grunted. "Not much more. Just got to get back to Megan. We're having guests."

Snow was in Linda's hair and on her shoulders. The light threw a pattern of pine needle shadows across her arm. Color was in her cheeks from the chill of a winter's day she had scarcely noticed. I never got my ride and it didn't matter. When a man loves his woman, and she shines like sunlight on the water, he's content to let things stand and just watch it happen.

She had prayed while she rode through the vast forest, she told me later. Dreamed. Sang songs. Felt that God was close and felt all that Christmas is supposed to mean—love, kindness, hope, Christ. A friend had come with nothing wrapped up, nothing purchased from Walmart or Sears, hands empty of any gift except a set of reins. Yet I cannot remember any other present from that day except the white horse and my wife of four years astride it in youth and perfection. In fact, in more than twenty-five years of marriage, it is one of the handful of Christmas gifts and experiences that stands out.

No man made the horse or wilderness my wife rode through. No man made the sun shine in the sky or the snow glitter at her feet. No man placed the bite of cold on her skin that made her feel alive and ready to snuggle up with a thick blanket when she got home. No man gave her the gift of prayer or faith she relished as the mare stepped through the green forest. But one man gave her the chance to experience all of that by a simple act of friendship.

Those are the days you take to your grave and, Lord willing, on into eternity.

19

Lion at the Chasm

Where is the dwelling of the lions, and the feeding-
place of the young lions, where the lion, even the
old lion, walked, and the lion's whelp, and none
made them afraid?

Nahum 2:11 KJV

It's one thing to enjoy the desert when you have plenty of
water, and another thing to view its mountains and buttes
when you are without water. It's one thing to take pleasure
in the sight of a powerful predator when you are safe from
attack, and another thing when that predator stands between
you and safety.

Many consider Roosevelt elk the most extraordinary elk
in the world. Vancouver Island has one of only two pure-
blood herds on the planet, and the racks the bulls sport are
enormous, frequently meeting or exceeding Safari Club International (SCI)and Boone and Crockett records. SCI and
Boone and Crockett are organizations that keep detailed

accounts of harvested animals of unusual size, including those who sport spectacular sets of antlers or horns. I never got a tag for one of the bulls, but Yukon, Nahanni, and I often tracked portions of the herd as it ranged the eastern forests of the Island. We would see them at a distance, turning their great necks to stare back at us, their buff coats and bright antlers in striking contrast to their dark heads. They never let us get too close before moving off.

Once, the three of us followed their prints farther into the Island's woods than we had ever gone before. It was impossible to miss a Roosevelt elk trail in wet or dry weather since the hooves left such large and deep impressions in mud or dirt. We wound up at the edge of a massive gorge crossed by a railroad bridge. The bridge was old and looked as if it had been put together with thousands of matchsticks. It had collapsed into the chasm one or two generations before, but its ends were surprisingly intact, as was some of the railway line that had been used to haul timber out of the rain forest.

Logging from another era was always evident when you hiked the interior of the Island. The dogs and I often came upon rusted blades curled in on themselves, the wooden handles into which they had once fit long gone. On rocky knolls we found campfires that had burned in the late 1800s or early 1900s, empty cans of beans in the dark coals with weathered labels, blue bottles with thick and square bottoms lying in the ash heaps along with brown ones for beer and, now and then, gray stoneware bottles as well. I wondered about the loggers who sat around those fires, felled great trees without power saws, risked death and brutal injury on a daily basis, saw huge elk, black bear, and cougar long before people had settled by the thousands into scores of coastal communities. What a different world it had been.

Yet, in some ways, not so different. The dense forests still kept towns and cities on the seacoasts, leaving the interior to the animals. The Island had never been hunted out of its wolves, cats, black-tailed deer, and Roosevelt elk. Gear forgotten a hundred years before remained where it was abandoned, untouched, rotting into the perpetual green, and though the old-time loggers with barrel chests and brawny shoulders and thick handlebar moustaches were gone, not so the Roosevelt elk or the black bears or bald eagles. Or, the cougars.

The scent at the chasm where we stopped in our pursuit of the elk herd was overpowering, as if a thousand tabby cats had sprayed inside a stairwell. No one needed to warn me a mountain lion had been here recently and was likely still in the vicinity. Yukon and Nahanni gave me a big-eyed look that said, "Are you sure we should be hanging around here?" When I indicated it was time to turn around they were on our back trail in an instant.

I told a friend about following the herd and he perked up, hands wrapped around a mug of Tim Hortons coffee.

"I've got a tag for a Roosevelt bull," Clark said. "How do I find that old logging road you were tracking them on?"

I sketched him a crude map, using landmarks only locals would understand, and told him he'd know he was in the right place when he came to the gorge and the broken railroad bridge.

"Something else," I warned as he scanned the map and asked questions. "The cougar scent there was pretty strong. I wasn't the only one trailing the herd."

Clark smiled. "I'm of the opinion the big cats keep to themselves if they're not molested. If one's around, he'll see me, but I'll never see him. I won't even know he's there."

A few days before the hunt opened up, my friend climbed in his truck and decided to go by four-wheel drive where I had gone by foot. Taking his time, now and then heading off on the wrong track, checking once or twice to see if there were still signs of elk, he made his way back into the thick green darkness of the Island forests. The gorge came suddenly and he braked. The collapsed bridge was obvious. He got out of his truck to look around.

The elk herd had not headed down into the chasm. The prints of dozens of animals, sinking deep into the damp earth and leaves of a west coast October, skirted the rim of the sharp drop-off and moved farther into the woods. He walked quietly in the same direction. After five minutes or so, he came to a clearing and could see elk hundreds of yards away, high up on a rocky slope. Several were bulls.

Careful not to step into the open, Clark lifted binoculars from where they hung about his neck and scanned what he could see of the herd for ten minutes or more. There were a number of places he felt he could get a shot at a bull from a different angle if he could commit himself to working slowly and painstakingly through the trees. Should the herd remain in the vicinity over the next week, he was confident of getting his pick of a fine Roosevelt elk. He began to head back to his truck.

Most of us have experienced a strong sense of personal danger at one time or another, even if we don't know what the danger is or where it is coming from. Some of us have sensed when our children or wife or friends were in trouble even though we were nowhere near them. Then there are times when it is more than an instinct, when it is almost like a voice speaking to us from within, and the voice is not our own, but feels supernatural or divine. My friend suddenly had both a gut feeling and a God feeling of danger and was immediately alert as he made his way through the forest.

Instead of rushing or walking upright, he almost crept. It seemed that God was warning him to be more cautious than usual. There was a strange combination of peace and fear in his mind. Bending down, he took a broken tree limb in his hands. It was thick and heavy. He did not have a gun with him, nor the large knife he often wore on his belt. The only thing he'd had on his mind when he climbed from the truck was scoping out elk. My advice about keeping his eyes open for cougar had been ignored. Yet just before he reached the pickup, he knew without a shadow of doubt that a big cat would be waiting for him.

It was over two hundred pounds. He made the estimation quickly as other parts of his brain went numb. The coat was already winter thick and shining. Tail twitching, like a long brown rope with a mind of its own, the cat stared him in the eye and did not look away. Clark lifted the tree limb in such a way he hoped the cat would take notice. He knew conventional wisdom was to fight a cat if it attacked, not play dead. Some people had driven them off with sticks and fishing rods. He also knew people had been killed doing that.

The strange mix of fear and peace remained in his mind. One part of him marveled that he was close enough to a mountain lion to practically count its whiskers. The other part was terrified the cat would pounce and break his skull open. But peace inexplicably ruled. He felt confident he would not be hurt. Confident enough that he began to advance upon the cat, brandishing his stout length of wood.

"Go on, go on," he growled in a low voice. "Get."

The cat was not cornered. It could move to the left or right—or straight at Clark. The steady approach and rumbling voice forced the lion to make a quick decision. It lowered its head and began to come forward. There was going to be a confrontation. Fear screamed inside Clark's mind, but the part that felt everything was under control calmed his spirit and kept him walking.

The cat suddenly veered to its left and went into the trees
and shadows. In moments, Clark could see nothing of the
cougar. Still, he faced the direction the cat had gone, holding his weapon chest high. Only when he had opened the
passenger door with one hand did he drop the tree limb and
jump into the truck. He leaned his head against the dash and
closed his eyes.

Boss Clay, hunter and avid outdoorsman, told me a man
always gets something out of the wilderness. There's always
a spiritual takeaway if you take the time to think about it.
For Clark, the day had been one of multiple blessings, as he
put it later. He'd found the Roosevelt elk, seen a cougar up
close for the first time in his life, and survived the encounter
with the cat, nary an injury. He had felt God's presence as
he faced down the big cat and was given the opportunity to
reflect on how a man deals with the different pressures and
challenges of life.

"Definitely, there are times you need to turn around and go
back and find another approach to the problem," he told me
over more Tim Hortons coffee. "And now and then, there's a
time to cut your losses and just get out of there—flee, really.
Because there's a good 'hanging in' and a bad 'hanging in'
and sometimes you have to make sure you live to fight another
day by disappearing."

He accepted a fresh cup of coffee from the waitress and
poured in some cream. "But neither of those approaches were
the right ones to use with the cougar and they're not always
the right ones to use in our lives either. Sometimes you have
to go at the problem head on, maybe not charge, but go at it
steady and sure—quitting or pulling back is not an option.
And that's how you win, by facing it down and never running."

"So how do you know which approach to take when?" I
prodded Clark. "What's the trick?"

He smiled as he sipped at his coffee. "The trick? To know yourself and know the instincts God puts inside you. And to know God's voice, when it really is him talking to you, telling you what moves to make. Know yourself. Know God. That's the trick."

"You make it sound so easy."

Clark set down the cup slowly. "It wasn't easy in the bush going head to head with a mountain lion and it isn't easy going head to head with tough issues on the job, or in the home, no matter what the problem is. Who said it had to be easy? It isn't about things being easy. It's about what you do being real. And it's about what you do being right, as right as you know how, by the grace of God."

20

The City That Burned to the Ground

> There are three things that are never satisfied, four
> that never say, "Enough!": the grave, the barren
> womb, land, which is never satisfied with water,
> and fire, which never says, "Enough!"
>
> Proverbs 30:15–16

They said later part of the problem was the deadwood on the hills and among the trees that should have been taken care of by controlled burns. Instead it was left to become fuel for the wildfire. It made me think of the deadwood in our own hearts and lives that we never take care of until it fuels a personal catastrophe.

Our home by the Rockies had seen hazy horizons and suns setting blood red for weeks. Fires had roared north from Montana through the backcountry, and our pass to hike and camp far inside Waterton Lakes National Park had been revoked.

Water bombers used a hill behind our house as a circling point for landing at the airstrip, and the World War II era snarl of Douglas A-26 Invaders made the air throb over our roof. I stood on the hill and watched the dark smoke boil out of the west and A-26s emerge from the maelstrom as if I were viewing air attacks over Germany in 1944 and 1945.

I drove with friends down to the airstrip, where it felt even more like a war zone. The aircraft roared in, took on fuel and fire retardant or water, and lifted off again toward the fires. I thought about my father, who in World War II had been a member of Bomber Command and based with the 427 Squadron in Leeming, Yorkshire. It was the only Canadian squadron to be sponsored by an American corporation—MGM Studios, because the 427 was the Lion Squadron. Dad had seen Wellingtons, Halifaxes, and Lancasters rumble along Runway 22 and head for military targets in Europe with much the same noise and hustle I was experiencing at the airstrip. Naming their bombers after MGM starlets like Joan Crawford, Lana Turner, and Greta Garbo, Dad's squadron had flown into the night to start fires on military targets while these A-26s flew into the dense clouds of smoke to put fires out. The fire fighting went on for so long near our home—with scorched pine needles spinning like black snow into our yard and each breath in our mouths tasting like ashes—that my wife and I decided to pack up the kids and head somewhere free of forest fires for a couple of weeks.

The Okanagan Valley in British Columbia has dry, Southern California-type terrain, minus palms and Joshua trees, strewn with lakes and fruit orchards and vineyards. When we phoned ahead to check on conditions, they told us the skies were clear, the sun bright, and the air clear of smoke—no forest fires were threatening. To get there we had to drive through areas that were definitely threatened—I watched spruce trees explode into flame on ridges high above us as we raced past on the highway. But once we reached the Okanagan, the sky really was crystal clear and free of smoke and ash. We settled happily into our rental house near the beach and slept like babies after our first swim in the lake.

Rather, I slept like a baby until about two in the morning. A loud boom of thunder woke me and I lay in the dark waiting to hear the sound of rain. It never came. A dry storm had swept through the region and moved on. In the morning there was only a faint plume of smoke on the far side of the lake from a lightning strike. I ignored it.

However, as the week carried on, the plume grew taller and darker and thicker—and closer. Some people we spoke with thought it was an issue, others didn't. Smoke began to obscure the blue sky and ashes began to drift down onto our heads, along with blackened spruce needles, just like back home. By the end of the week, fire fighting had intensified and people were streaming out of the city, pickups piled high with belongings. The bridge south was jammed and traffic hardly moved.

The great pillar of smoke was at the edge of the city and I had an eerie feeling I was in a war zone again where people were fleeing not a wildfire, but an invading army of soldiers and armored vehicles. I imagined tanks clanking along the asphalt streets, their long snouts swinging back and forth, ready to fire, turning houses to rubble with their shells and sending flame and smoke skyward. The mood in the city became more and more grim, and my wife and I thought it might be time to cut our vacation short and make plans to move out.

Hesitant, we decided to call the mayor's office and volunteer to help in any way we could, but the city said they had more than enough volunteers. A wind soon sprang up. The sky was still an ugly gray, but we took our son and daughter to the beach to body surf, perhaps the last time they would get to enjoy the lake. It was a wonderful time for them, the waves big and warm, their small boards scooting over the water, the two of them laughing with more abandon than they had in days under the death cloud of smoke and ash. But the wind that gave them surf whipped the wilderness fire into a frenzy.

A strange quiet came over the city that night. The bridge was still in gridlock, but hundreds gathered on beaches to watch red and orange flames shoot high into the blackness as the fire that had swallowed vineyards and orchards now devoured homes and buildings. Men, women, and children had been evacuated from the neighborhoods in the disaster zone, but fire fighters were in great danger as they tried to stop a monster blaze the wind had churned into a hurricane of heat and destruction. Houses exploded—the whole horizon would ignite in a sudden overpowering flash as one after another went up. I recalled footage I had seen of the London Blitz.

If the wind shifted or gained in strength the city core would be threatened—which meant my wife, my children, and I, as well as tens of thousands of others, would have to get out as quickly as possible. But how could anyone get across a bridge already crammed with refugees? The lake was shallow, you could wade for hundreds of yards, so I made up my mind I would take my family out as far as we could go to escape a blaze set to tear through the beachfront homes and downtown like a predator.

Strangers talked to strangers in hushed tones. I spoke with people I'd never met, and would never meet again, about what we might do, where we might go, what might happen if the winds rose and pushed the wall of fury our way. Of course, my wife and I prayed. I expect many people prayed, including those who never prayed. Certainly the city's churches were praying as well as sending cards and videos of support to the fire fighters who were risking their lives. Grave danger made people reach for help not only from other humans they would normally have never said two words to, but also from a God they never had the slightest intention of saying any words to at all.

It was impossible to sleep. Micah and Micaela eventually dropped off to sleep despite this night of flame and wind. Linda was at the house with them, while I paced the beach and watched the night break apart in balls of fire. Finally, I returned and succumbed to exhaustion on a couch in the front room with a window open, ready to jump up if I heard evacuation sirens or police pounding on the door.

At dawn I stepped outside. The wind was gone, the horizon no longer roiling with smoke and fire. A call to the people who had rented us the house confirmed the immediate threat was over unless the winds started up again. Sunlight trickled over the rooftops and sidewalks and the smell of burnt things hung in the air like ravens.

No lives were lost, but plenty of fire fighters came close and had stories to tell of miraculous escapes from situations in which they were completely encircled by fires. Well over two hundred homes vanished in sheets of flame and blasts of heat and light. Thousands were emotionally drained—the fire had leaped over some homes without touching them, while demolishing others, leaving many neighborhoods with people who were elated along with people who were devastated. The threat was not completely gone, so trucks and cars still moved bumper to bumper over the narrow bridge. We stayed on and spent another week in the city as it gradually began to recover and listened to TV broadcasts where explanations were sought and blame apportioned.

Decades of dry wood, fallen trees and branches, stuff that could have been removed from the hills and forests around the city and not permitted to accumulate, had helped feed the fire until it grew to enormous and unstoppable proportions. In the same way, broken attitudes, dry spirits, and brittle hurts within ourselves can feed anger and resentment until they explode into fury and bitterness. Praying, confessing faults, forgiving others and asking forgiveness, worshiping, Bible reading, and sharing in Christian friendship can help remove a lot of the deadfall in our hearts and souls. This needs to be done before a lightning strike of disappointment, or the spark of crisis, makes matters worse by causing unresolved issues to burst into flame.

Adding even more combustible material to the fires of the present can create situations that result in domestic abuse, divorce, broken friendships, broken churches, estrangement from our children, and even criminal charges. Lives and families and Christian communities that once knew peace and safety can burn to the ground. Whole worlds of love and strength can go up in smoke. The wise maintain their hunting firearms and ammunition so that using them will not be hazardous. Seasoned hikers take care of their boots and sleeping bags and tents so that none of their gear will fail if a storm hits in a wilderness setting. In the same way, so Christians must keep heart, spirit, and mind free of things that clog and obstruct, praying out and working through anything that poses danger to ourselves and those we love before it's too late.

21

Buffalo Stampede

Ask which paths are the old, reliable paths. Ask which way leads to blessings. Live that way.

Jeremiah 6:16 GOD'S WORD

But my people are not so reliable, for they have deserted me. . . . They have stumbled off the ancient highways and walk in muddy paths.

Jeremiah 18:15 NLT

The American bison or buffalo is a magnificent creature in solitary, but a herd stampeding over the prairie is even more of a majestic sight—provided they are moving away from you rather than straight at you.

The buffalo was on American nickels from 1913 to 1938, and it still remains the symbol of the Canadian province of Manitoba as well as the state animal of Wyoming, Oklahoma, and Kansas. It is also at the center of the crest of the

147

red-coated Royal Canadian Mounted Police. As far as I'm concerned, it would be entirely appropriate for it to be the symbol of Canada rather than the beaver or the maple leaf. The great bison's range once extended from northern Canada to Durango, Mexico, as well as to the western Rocky Mountains and east to the Appalachians. There were 40 million buffalo at the peak of their population. One of the last two continuously wild buffalo herds runs free in northern Alberta at Wood Buffalo National Park, where selective hunting is permitted to keep the population at a healthy level.

Where we live, buffalo once thrived not by the thousands or tens of thousands, but the millions. When a foundation for a new house was dug just across the street from us, the kids came back with bags of buffalo bones. On dirt trails I often find bison jawbones, which I place on my workbench. A friend was romping with his dog in some tall grass and gullies nearby when he stumbled upon a buffalo skull, complete with unbroken horns, sitting in the dirt, far from human eyes. It had been resting there for close to 150 years. Our region saw the big herds graze under the shadow of the Rocky Mountains, and our neighborhood saw them stream down to the creek for a drink. If only our big old cottonwood trees, a number of which were standing in the 1840s and 1850s, could talk.

I've been around buffalo herds all my life. A wild bull can easily weigh in at a ton and a domestic one can tip the scales at 3,000 pounds or more. They are short tempered and unpredictable and will attack humans in a flash. You cannot outrun them, as slow and ponderous as they may seem, because bison reach speeds of 40 miles an hour. In the last two decades of the twentieth century, they injured nearly three times as many people as bears in Yellowstone National Park. Not far from my home, and not that many months ago, a man from out of town was visiting friends and went for an early morning walk in the woods and fields. He encountered a buffalo bull that was grazing and felt threatened by his presence. The bull charged and gored the man, killing him. It was a huge shock to his family and our community.

I have viewed bison from my vehicle in several states and provinces, most of the time within parks or buffalo preserves, but sometimes on private ranches where they are raised and slaughtered for the commercial sale of their meat. The truth is, I don't feel all that safe in a car or truck moving among buffalo, let alone anywhere near them on foot. As my wife and I drove slowly through a preserve once with the kids, the herd chose to gather tightly around us, and it was pretty unnerving. I knew a large bull could push his head and bulk against our vehicle and roll it easily, the same way a hippo or elephant or water buffalo could do it at an African game park. So, making every effort not to provoke the bulls, I stopped our Cherokee and we just sat there.

The small herd shambled away from where we were parked and began to form up a few hundred feet off the dirt track. Suddenly I realized the bulls were putting the calves and cows behind them and setting up a ring. They faced outward with their heads and horns, defying us and protecting the females and young. Some of the horns were two feet long. It was fascinating to watch them set up their defensive circle, but it was also clear to me that I never wanted to be on the business end of those powerful horns.

When Micah and Micaela were young, there was a buffalo paddock only a few miles from our house. You could open the gate, drive in, make your way around the enclosure and find the herd, then latch the gate on your way out. One day I brought the whole family there, including my brother and his wife. The gate was locked, but a quick search found an open walk-in farther down the fence line. Normally, upon entering the main gate, you still had another enclosure to go through before getting into the buffalo area proper, so I led our group into the first paddock confidently, my son riding on my shoulders.

The walk was amazing. The grass was tall, green, and luxuriant. Wildflowers glittered blue, purple, and yellow everywhere we looked, rising high from the earth and grass. The reason for all the healthy growth was the huge number of buffalo pies strewn from one end of the field to the other. Acting like natural fertilizer, they had stimulated growth in the prairie grass and flowers, flowers that were far larger than the ones I was used to seeing on mountain slopes or in the foothills. Many spiked through the dung on top of them and kept going. Bees and wasps hummed loudly. There wasn't ten feet anywhere that wasn't littered with buffalo droppings. It forced us to take our steps in a more creative manner.

"This is something!" my brother, Bill, exclaimed. "Now we know what the Great Plains looked like in the early 1800s after a large herd had grazed through a region."

"Yeah," I agreed. "And we also know how the pioneers found enough of this stuff to use for cooking fires when there weren't sticks or branches."

I had never seen anything like it. The tall flowers, high grass, and buffalo dung extended for miles in all directions. I could imagine wagon trains creaking through the grass, finally coming to a stop for the night, and children being sent to help collect pies that were dry and solid. Piled together, they were ignited by the use of tinder and flint. Water was boiled, potatoes and meat cooked, bread baked. Any buffalo still in the vicinity would be harvested for food, lean cuts smoked and dried over the dung fire, the scent of cooking flesh mingling with the distinctive smell of the buffalo chips—sometimes like straw and dry grass, sometimes, strangely, a Christmas aroma of cloves and cinnamon.

"How big is this herd?" Bill's wife, Talia, asked. "There seem to be an awful lot of buffalo chips here."

"Well, it's not huge," I told her. "I think they must have been put in this paddock for a few weeks before they were moved back into their regular enclosure."

"So they're not in this part?"

I shook my head, Micah still riding on my shoulders as I held his ankles. "There's another gate. Look at the pies. They're all dry. White and gray. Not one of them is moist."

Five minutes after I said this to Talia, I almost stepped in a pie that was brown and speckled with what looked like semi-digested clover. It wasn't fresh by any means—its edges had hardened and blackened. Still, bluebottles buzzed around and landed one after another on its surface. A minute or so later there was a second brown pie. Then a third. It gave a man cause to wonder where exactly the herd might be. A few minutes after stumbling upon a fourth pie, I found out.

Micah and I had gotten ahead of the group, thoroughly enjoying ourselves and the sunny day. In front of us appeared a grove of sturdy shade trees with wide-spreading branches thick with leaves. Underneath the trees were dozens of large dark shapes. Before we had a chance to take this in, birds lifted from the trees in a burst of flapping wings and wheeled into the sun. Then the shapes under the trees exploded.

Dust flew. Heavy branches that had fallen to the ground spun into the air as hooves smacked down. The horns were obvious, as was the great girth of the beasts. Panic was in their eyes—rolled back white. The ground was shaking. The buffalo were close . . . and coming right at us.

They filled my ears with thunder, and for a few seconds all I could see were the humps, the hair, and the horns. There was nowhere for me to go, nowhere for my family to hide; the land was flat and wide open for miles. Only three or four dozen stampeded toward us, hooves pounding the grass and dirt, but it might as well have been a thousand. Fear crashed through my mind and body.

Where could we run? Where could we turn? I remained frozen to the spot, Micah high on my shoulders. There was a dry gulch between us and the buffalo herd, but I didn't know if it would make any difference. The lead bulls stared wild-eyed at Micah and I and then stared wild-eyed at the shallow gulch that ran between the herd and my family. In a finger snap, they veered, dust and dirt continuing to boil up from their hooves like gray smoke. Pouring over the grass in the opposite direction, they headed for a nearby butte. Once the herd reached it, they streamed out of sight behind its brown and green bulk. I'd been totally surprised to find them under the shade trees, frightened when they stampeded, and relieved when they changed direction and vanished. From one thing to the next, all of it had taken place in less than half a minute.

The group of us looked at one another.

"That's something you don't see every day," Bill said.

"Good thing," his wife responded.

"Imagine a million of them."

Micah and Micaela had eyes as big and bright as suns.

"I guess," I mumbled, almost to myself, "I will make a practice of not walking into buffalo paddocks anymore, even if a gate is open."

I have never forgotten the flowers growing through the buffalo chips on each side of me that day, grass that was almost too green, buffalo that roared over the land like a brown and black torrent. Somehow, when I recall all that, I grip hands with both pioneers and Native Americans who saw the great herds and wide-open spaces before both disappeared forever.

One gift of the wilderness is its ability to hold you suspended in time, as if yesterday and tomorrow do not exist. Another gift is its ability to take you back in time—you find old campfires, long discarded logging tools from another era, a herd of wild horses in a canyon, bison thundering across the plains as if it is still 1845.

God has a way of taking me back in time when I read the Bible so that I am in those lands and among those people and make their struggles of faith my own despite the fact that they lived and died thousands of years before I was born. The Bible also has a way of taking me back into my own past and showing me things I had forgotten, good and bad, so that I have cause to both thank God as well as open my heart to him so it can be scrubbed clean. Past experiences become present realties as God goes back in time to illuminate matters that make the present easier to live with and the future easier to walk into. Where good things ran free in my heart, they can run free again, where space for God's Spirit has been choked off, the way can be cleared and space opened up once more. Where I used to walk in great liberty with Jesus Christ, any loss of that liberty can be restored so that I am a man alive, not one half dead.

The wilderness often mirrors so much of what happens inside a man—tough slopes, rough waters, and fierce mountain winds symbolize hard and painful life passages, while clear skies at a peak's summit, smooth green rivers, and a warm campfire at night symbolize the opposite.

The wild is not only a place for physical and emotional renewal. It is one of God's chosen instruments for coming to grips with what has damaged our souls, so that our spirits can be revitalized and the whole world made new, whether by prayer and repentance, or by praise and thankfulness. It is where the words of God can strike home without the distractions of work and traffic and wide screen TVs. For a while, past, present, and future all become one as we spend quality time with a Friend who is eternal and who lives outside the boundaries and restrictions of clocks and calendars.

I always take a Bible with me into the wild places so that I can hear God's voice in a fresh way among the streams and peaks and slanting bars of light. I have two Bibles that are bound in buckskin; others are small enough to fit in a coat pocket. One is a different translation from the other. It doesn't matter. I've found God is able to get through to me regardless of which translation I use. He can hit home with Greek and Hebrew and Aramaic as well as a Bible designed for a grade 4 reading level.

In a wilderness both ancient and new, with holy words from a Bible both ancient and new, experienced by human life that also consists of what is ancient and new, I hear what I had once known, but had forgotten, and am told secrets never known that make my spirit leap and put fresh strength in my heart. The old ways of God, which are forever new, make me a new man.

Thomas Merton put it this way:

> By reading the scriptures I am so renewed that all nature seems renewed around me and with me. The sky seems to be a pure, a cooler blue, the trees a deeper green. The whole world is charged with the glory of God and I feel fire and music under my feet.[3]

3. Thomas Merton, *The Sign of Jonas* (New York: Harcourt, Brace & Co., 1953), 215–216.

22

Skunk Tails

There's an opportune time to do things, a right
time for everything on the earth: . . . A right time
to cry and another to laugh.

Ecclesiastes 3:1, 4 THE MESSAGE

Sometimes, as the Bible says, we laugh at one moment and
cry at another. But sometimes we just have to laugh and cry
at the same time.

It seems everyone has a skunk story, whether they've camped
out in the bush or not. At the very least, we've all driven past
a dead one on the highway. A good number of us, of course,
have had close encounters of the black and white kind at our
cottages, our tents, our RVs, or just strolling along a trail in
the evening. Not too many, though, can tell a story about a
family of skunks trying to set up shop in their living room!

All my dogs have been skunked at least once. It goes with
the territory—if you live close to the woods, dog and skunk

are bound to meet. But one spring, the dogs were getting skunked more than usual. I wasn't sure what was bringing the black and whites into our yard in record numbers. Opening the door from the garage to the dog run one night, Yukon and Nahanni crowding me from behind, I flicked on the outside light and caught a young skunk in its beam. The skunk froze, terrified, its hair spiking, its tail rising. Equally surprised . . . and terrified, I promptly slammed the door, dogs protesting.

"Forget it!" I snapped. "No one goes into that run tonight!"

A day later, one of the physicians my wife works with was jogging on the other side of the creek from our house when he saw a parade of young skunks proudly following their mother along the path that skirts our property.

"There were seven of them," he told my wife when he got back to the clinic. "Eight, counting the mother."

"Did you see where they came from?" she asked.

"No. But my guess is they're hanging out in your neighborhood."

A week after the doctor's sighting we had a team up from Mississippi and Louisiana to help our church with youth work. A couple approached me after the end of a busy day in our large backyard and said they had seen seven or eight skunks marching along the creek bank.

"Really?" I responded as if it was the first time I'd heard of skunks. "Did they head on into the bush?"

Both of them had a worried look. The man cleared his throat. "Well, they all ended up under your deck."

This was a cause for alarm. Had the skunks only stayed for the night or had they taken up permanent residence? I was not yet desperate enough to crawl under the deck with a flashlight and find out for sure, so I called the town to ask them to set up a live trap. The town's policy at that time was to give me the trap and walk away.

"Use tuna," they told me. "Skunks love tuna. Of course, cats love it too. You might catch quite a few cats before you get a skunk."

What about getting sprayed? No, if the skunk was in the trap properly it wouldn't be able to lift its tail. What about releasing it if I caught one? Would they at least help with that? No, it was up to me to take the skunk somewhere safe and release it and return the trap to them.

"Hey, be careful when you release it," they warned me. "You don't want it to turn on you. Skunks carry rabies."

Okay . . . that settled that. I decided to shelf the trap idea for the time being. But I had to do something.

One week later I was in the laundry room and happened to glance out the window onto the back deck. Little creatures were rooting around among the flowers growing in our planter. Little black and white creatures. I quickly closed the window to seal off the screen. The noise made them jump and they began chittering and milling about. Then they crawled down into a hole in the planter, one after another, still chittering in distress, and disappeared. I was brave enough to examine the hole a few hours later. It led, as I suspected it must, underneath the deck.

Bringing the dogs back from their walk the next evening, the three of us were treated to an astonishing sight: a mob of small skunks were running and tumbling and tussling in the thick grass of our backyard. Soon they headed into our garden and jumped around among the raspberry canes and herbs and perennials. We watched the plants shake and the leaves tremble. I called the town the next day.

"Well," they said, "you have to remember the skunk is a member of the wolverine family. They're pretty smart. If they're in your garden they're doing nothing but good—eating up grubs and pests and slugs and beetles."

"But what about them spraying my dogs?"

"Well, we still got a trap here with your name on it. But they're doing nothing but good in your garden, nothing but good."

The smell of musk that lingered around certain parts of the deck during the summer convinced me that the skunk family never moved on. It was true that I had to haul out the Zest and tomato juice and lime juice less and less to scrub down the dogs, but I knew the skunks were still lurking in our yard, still living under our deck, and still getting fat on our grubs. They had us surrounded. The ultimate shock came when I was working in the kitchen and saw movement on the deck by the back door. The door was basically one long pane of glass so it was easy to see the black and white tails fluttering and the heads and paws moving back and forth.

I crept to the door. The babies had grown up. If mother had been doing most of the spraying in May and June, it was clear her daughters and sons could hold their own in July and August. I hid behind the freestanding pantry so they could not see me—the last thing I wanted was a well-sprayed deck. What were they up to? Catching flies? Eating spiders? My blood froze. They were trying to open the door.

One of them had its claws in the crack between door and doorframe and was making every effort to pry. When it gave up, another one took its place. And another. They were skittering and chittering and tumbling over one another in their eagerness to get inside and ransack my cupboards and shelves. And if they could get an unlocked back door open, why couldn't they pry open a fridge as well?

I imagined coming home one afternoon, walking through the front door, suddenly taking in a lungful of spray, and collapsing on the floor, gagging. From this position, I would see jam, peanut butter, flour, pastrami, milk, and ketchup covering the walls and carpets and tiles. The skunk family would be hunkered down in the middle of the living room, tearing open an assortment of cracker boxes, packages of deli meat, and bags of rice. When I tried to get up they would spot the movement, grow alarmed, and all spray at once. Finished with that horrifying vision, I went to the town hall and picked up a trap.

I placed it in a prominent location near the back deck and baited it with an open tin of light tuna. I checked it each morning. Unfortunately, the skunks ignored the trap. So did the neighborhood cats. No one expressed any interest except the local flies. When the stench of three-day-old tuna began to foster a revolt in the family, I dispatched the tuna to the trash can and returned the trap to the town.

Nothing else happened. Fall arrived. No more sprayings, no more sightings. It felt to me like the circus had moved on to another town. The dogs ran freely in the yard, echinacea opened up in the garden, and I grew brave enough to crawl under the deck on my hands and knees and take a look around—a lingering scent was in the air, but nothing else.

Our guest room backs onto the deck. One day I was fixing something in the washroom when I heard the rustling of autumn leaves, not from the window, but under my feet. It sounded exactly like a creature circling before bedding down. With the noise came a scent, faint, but distinctly unpleasant. It seemed to me I had smelled this before in years past and had chalked it up to something moldy in the closet. Now I wondered if somebody might not have a perpetual hibernation nest under the deck, snug against the foundation of our house. I decided to make another call to the town.

With the coming of winter, the mayor and councilors had decided on a change of skunk trap policy. What incident occurred to bring this about I have no idea, but now the peace officers would set the traps and deal with the release of the black and whites. So another trap was placed by our deck and baited with tuna. At first, all was quiet. The trap was still empty when I went to bed at midnight.

Early the next morning I was walking my dogs on the opposite side of the creek from our home. I could see the trap from where I stood. To my surprise, the gate to the cage was shut and something was moving around inside, something big. I hurried over the bridge and half ran to the house with the dogs at my side.

I still didn't trust the promise that skunks couldn't spray inside one of the traps, but I locked the dogs in their run, snuck up, and took a look anyways. It was the mother of all skunks—I was certain it was a female—and she wasn't very pleased with the way things had turned out after her tuna surprise. I almost felt sorry for her as a bylaw officer arrived to cart her away, crowing in triumph at his catch and confirming that she was indeed a female.

"Biggest one we've hauled in all year," he said with a grin. "I'll bet she's mothered a hundred of them."

"Do you think the brood I saw was hers?" I asked.

"Probably."

"Where are they?"

"On their own now."

Sometimes they euthanized the skunks, especially if they were dealing with an explosion in numbers or a rabies epidemic. In this case, they took the grand old lady west to the mountains and let her go, opening the trap with a cord while they sat in the truck. She made her way into the woods, no doubt found a suitable den under a tree or boulder, and settled in for the winter. The faint and disagreeable scent disappeared from the guest room and has never returned. I've seen skunks again, of course, but never seven or eight at a time living under my deck. I suppose that had been the mother's nesting place for years and had become something of a home. When spring returned, I worried that her sons and daughters would return with it. But they never did, at least not to take up permanent residency in record numbers.

An old girlfriend once told me she knew God had a sense of humor because he had created bumblebees. A friend from Australia had made the same declaration of faith based on the existence of the platypus: the bill of a duck, the feet of an otter, the tail of a beaver, the only mammal that lays eggs—and venomous. Others find sea otters hilarious, dolphins playful, and the young of all species an entertainment—calves, foals, kittens, puppies, you name it.

Even skunks are evidence of God's boundless humor. As annoying as the spraying that summer had been, I couldn't deny the energy and enthusiasm of those young kin of the wolverine. As I watched them tumble in the grass or romp through the garden, I often thought how pleasant it would be to have them around if only they didn't have those glands. But that is their protection, like quills for the porcupine, teeth for the wolf, and talons for the hawk. A pretty secure protection too, in many ways more effective than fangs or claws or strength, all of which predators have learned to overcome. It's hard to overcome the stench of skunk spray, though, and few would want to eat the carcass that would be at their disposal even if they did.

Skunks bring to mind things that are less than lovely, the kinds of things God uses regardless of their lack of popularity or lack of beauty. Skunks are not seen as desirable, yet they made my garden healthy—pests were eliminated and the raspberry crop was rich. Some experiences in life are hard and bitter, yet they teach us things not only about ourselves and our world, but also about our God that are far brighter and more hopeful than the harsh experiences themselves. Things that seem insignificant turn out to be more important than the bigger events we thought everything hinged upon.

This all sounds like Paul when he sat down to write his first letter to the Christians in the city of Corinth: "God has chosen the foolish things of the world to shame the wise, and God has chosen the weak things of the world to shame the things which are strong" (1 Corinthians 1:27 NASB).

It also sounds a lot like the way Paul describes the assortment of people who make up the churches we attend, comparing the church to the various parts of the human body. He says that everyone and everything—even the things most minuscule and the people who attract the least attention and get the least praise—have their place in God's plan and God's kingdom:

> Some parts of the body that seem weakest and least important are actually the most necessary. And the parts we regard as less honorable are those we clothe with the greatest care. So we carefully protect those parts that should not be seen, while the more honorable parts do not require this special care. So God has put the body together such that extra honor and care are given to those parts that have less dignity. This makes for harmony among the members, so that all the members care for each other. If one part suffers, all the parts suffer with it, and if one part is honored, all the parts are glad. All of you together are Christ's body, and each of you is a part of it.
>
> 1 Corinthians 12:22–27 NLT

Regardless of which animals and birds we personally take pleasure in and which we don't, God made them all, he called them good, and they all fit into what he is doing in the world.

"Thou art worthy, O Lord, to receive glory and honor and power: for thou hast created all things, and for thy pleasure they are and were created" (Revelation 4:11 KJV).

23

Bush Camp

He sends the snow like white wool; he scatters
frost upon the ground like ashes. He hurls the
hail like stones. Who can stand against his freez-
ing cold?

Psalm 147:16–17 NLT

The job was to do security at a northern bush camp. The camp
and its men were there to put up a hydroelectric dam to supply
power to the towns and cities in the region. It was easier to
work in the winter because the bitter cold froze the swamps
and muskeg solid, allowing trucks and heavy equipment to do
their work without becoming mired or sinking out of sight.
Security was there to make sure there was no vandalism or
sabotage and to keep the men safe—safe from outsiders and
safe from each other when the winter grew too long and too
dark and the workers felt too isolated and too confined.

So I took the job. I had never been so close to the Arctic
Circle. Sure, it was still hundreds of miles away, but the region

I was in shared many similar traits with the Arctic. Polar bears were close by, the pine trees were stunted, the swamp and muskeg and lakes frozen stiff. Everything was hard as iron in the absolute cold. Trucks could use winter roads built on the ice of lakes and rivers, while heavy machinery could carve out the massive pit for a reservoir and hydroelectric dam. I had been hired on with a group of others to keep hundreds of workers out of harm's way and under control—I was security with a uniform and badge, but no gun.

Why would a nineteen-year-old do it? The money was good, and when saved up would enable me to eventually fulfill a dream of traveling around the world. I was always looking for adventure, and heading into a northern bush camp seemed a perfect opportunity. But I should have thought about the sharp drop in temperature from southern Canada. And I should have thought about the kind of men the pay at a northern bush camp attracts and what a winter in isolation can do to the strongest of wills.

Even our routine introduction to the task at hand held a hint of menace. The sergeant walked us up and down the barren halls of the long trailers where workers ate, relaxed, and slept. We patrolled the bleak grounds in a heavy truck. There were checkpoints where we turned keys in the slot of the heavy time boxes we carried to prove we had completed our patrolling rounds. The sergeant warned us that a security guard at another camp had recently been murdered when an unknown assailant struck him on the head with his own time box and left the body lying in the snow.

The sergeant pointed out the men from Northern Ireland he claimed worked for the IRA: "They send their paychecks back home to help the terrorist cause." Nothing had been proven, but officials had their suspicions. RCMP showed up regularly and checked the files of all employees—truck drivers, heavy equipment operators, electricians, mechanics, cooks—to see if they could spot wanted criminals. Sometimes they found felons who were on the run or men who had skipped out on parole, and arrested them. But sometimes they missed them.

"They gain weight or lose it," an RCMP constable explained to me as he eyed the men at other tables as we ate lunch. "Grow beards or shave them off. Wear glasses. Stay out of the way when police show up. Where else can they make money like this and have free food and a place to live and be out of sight of the law?"

He told me to watch my back. Some of the men that hid out under false identities in the camps were wanted murderers or violent offenders. If they thought I had suspicions about them, they would not hesitate to crack my skull open with my time box, or break my neck from behind, or slip a knife between my ribs. Who would ever know who did it in the cold winter dark of early morning?

How many wanted men passed through the camp that winter I'll never know. I tried to get along with everyone and give a hand where a hand was needed. Be a good cop. But there were still the hard calls. Sometimes men would throw a party in their room that was so loud and raucous, security had to deal with it. A lot of these men were big and rough and it was no easy task to knock on the door, have them open it drunk and reckless, and ask them, and oftentimes order them, to turn the music down and stop the shouting.

The poker games in the rooms were the worst. Men who earned four or five thousand a week would sign their paychecks and toss them into the pot, usually losing it all. Many who didn't use direct deposit had three or four checks in their wallet at any given time. If they were drunk enough, they might throw them all in. A man who woke up the morning after and came to the realization he had bet twenty thousand dollars the night before and lost every penny of it was not a man you wanted to be around. But if he went berserk, my partners and I had to deal with it.

Not much more than a year before, I'd been playing high school football. Slender and slick, I'd been nicknamed Tooth-pick. Now at the camp I began to lift weights and eat more protein to bulk up. Deciding I needed a more fierce presence, I cut my hair off. All of it. Friends used shaving cream and a razor to take it right down to the skin. So there I was with a shining dome atop my head.

The weight training and hair loss worked. The next time I boarded the bus bringing new employees into camp, the driver whipped the fur hat with the badge from my head—and suddenly there I was, six four, gaining muscle, with a naked head and absolutely no smile. The men on the bus reacted as one, each of them narrowing their eyes and giving me a worried look at the same time.

"Welcome to camp," I greeted the busload. "Do any of you have any firearms to declare?"

"Man, you're a big one, ain't you?" one of the men responded. "You can have whatever you like so long as you leave me alone."

After the drinking parties and poker games, the worst case scenarios were Dear John letters. A man came to security in a panic one night and told us his roommate had received a letter from his girlfriend breaking off their relationship. Now he was cutting himself up with a razor blade. We ran to his room.

There was already blood all over his chest and his sheets as he lay on his bed, carving up his skin. Quickly I began talking to distract him as the corporal edged toward the bed. Suddenly he grabbed the razor blade from the man's hand. I thought there would be a fight, but the man was too drunk and had lost too much blood. He was patched up as best as our medic could and was sent out for stitches. He needed seventy-eight of them.

It's not that there weren't occasional moments of friendship, good laughter (particularly during film nights), or kindness from one man to another. Christians met and prayed, Bibles were read, Christmas decorations put up, guitars picked up, and songs sung.

But I was in security, and when you're in security you always get the dirty work. You are the one who has to break up fistfights. You wrestle big men back to their rooms when they are drunk and disorderly. You ignore those who try to provoke conflict by turning their plates of food upside down after squashing cigarette butts into scrambled eggs or steak. You order rugged individuals to lay down their Bowies and switchblades and stop their knife fight. You do it twelve hours a day, seven days a week, with two weeks back home every three months.

When it dropped to sixty below one day, I pulled my truck over to watch the dawn instead of running inside for a hot breakfast—the intense cold made the colors more brilliant and etched every tree and blue jay and snowdrift in sharp and precise detail. Beauty. With so much ugliness in the camp, I wanted to see beauty. The stars had been like crushed diamonds during the icy black night. Now the sun set the world on fire and the sky throbbed blue and gold. *Just like God*, I thought, *to show so much beauty where so few humans see it. And those who could see it, if they made the effort, are huddled indoors and indifferent.*

I did not stay inside the truck, though I did leave the engine running. I stepped out, walked into the woods a few yards, and took a painful breath of the arctic air into my lungs.

Smelled the pine. The light was pouring over the snow like golden syrup, and above, vivid sapphire and azure colored the beautiful sky.

The cold was life threatening. It made it hard to work, difficult to run vehicles and equipment. Yet it also brought out an energy and richness in nature that mild temperatures did not. Men might be doing hard things to themselves and one another in the camp; terrorists might be mailing their paychecks back home so that others could purchase guns and bombs. But God's wilderness was still beautiful despite all those things and despite the frost that stung my cheeks and nose. In the middle of my long dark winter, God was still God, and the snowflake and pine needle and bird feather and sun still came from his hand, regardless of what evil men might do.

"God never made an ugly landscape," wrote John Muir. "All that sun shines on is beautiful, so long as it is wild."[1]

This was good to remember, because that night I was given the worst assignment of my winter in the far north. The sergeant called me into his office and asked me to shut the door. He waited until it clicked. I thought I was in for a dressing down.

"Look," he said, "a message was left for Mike Stedham. He needs to call home."

I hesitated. "Stedham? That's it? You want me to tell him to call home?"

The sergeant stared at me. "You have to prepare him for the news. They wanted us to tell him so he was ready when he phoned his mother and father."

"Tell him what?"

"His brother's been electrocuted. He was making a repair to a power line with his crew down south. Something went wrong."

1. *Atlantic Monthly,* January 1869.

I felt cold. "He's in the hospital."

"All the voltage went through him. He's dead. Take Stedham aside and let him know that before he picks up the phone."

"Stedham hates my guts."

"Stedham hates every cop's guts."

I walked out of the office and found Stedham eating supper in the dining hall with his buddies. A tough bunch. Always spoiling for a fight. I and my partners had wrestled him and his pals back to their rooms when they were drunk and flailing with their fists on several occasions. I prayed for words and approached the table. Stedham looked up from his plate, scowling as I drew near.

"What is it?" he snapped.

"Mr. Stedham, I need to have a minute with you."

"What for?"

"There's something I have to tell you."

"If you got something to tell me you can say it right here. I'm not going anywhere with you."

"Please, Mr. Stedham—"

He put down his fork and knife. "I'm not kidding," he growled. "Say what you got to say and then walk away."

There was nothing I could do. I leaned across the table so that my face was closer to his and I lowered my voice. "Mike. Your father and mother called Security. They wanted you to phone home after we relayed the message."

His face suddenly tightened. "What message?"

"Your brother was fixing a power line. There was an accident. He was electrocuted. He's dead, Mike. I'm sorry."

Mike Stedham read my eyes and saw I was telling him exactly what I knew. He looked around the table at his friends. They had all heard. They had all stopped eating. He pushed himself up and walked into the hall where a number of pay phones were located.

At dawn, I finished my rounds in the trailers and headed out to the truck. It was still sixty below and taking a breath made me wince. But all around me was God's wild, where the sky was turning a vivid blue and the last stars were almost as big and bright as the noon sun. I was about to climb behind the wheel when I spotted a man standing in the forest a hundred feet away. He wore a parka and his back was to me. He was crying.

I waited, unsure what to do. Finally he turned around. It was Mike. He knew I could see his tears but didn't care. I remained standing by the truck. He came toward me slowly over the snow. Once he reached my side he stopped. His eyes were swollen. He shifted his gaze to the sunrise.

"Sometimes this is all we got, kid," he said quietly. "You'll find out as you get older. My brother and I fished together and hunted together. Now the wilderness is all I've got left. I love it. We both loved it. It's all I have now that reminds me of him. It's all I have that makes sense of anything in this crazy life."

I was going to speak but he held up his hand.

"Take it easy," he said.

Then he walked past me and took a trail that wound about the trailers and eventually headed east across a frozen lake. As the sun rose higher I had to squint as I watched him go. He vanished in the brilliant light.

"Help him," I prayed. "Thank you that what you made without human hands is here this morning and just as incredible as it was when his brother was still alive."

Muir had written that "in God's wildness lies the hope of the world."[2] In my mind I changed it to, "In Christ and in God's wildness lies the hope of the world." No matter what

2. John Muir, *John of the Mountains: The Unpublished Journals of John Muir* (Madison, WI: The University of Wisconsin Press, 1979), 317.

we experience, he is there, and a wilderness he made that can do us so much good, and rearrange our skewed thinking, is there too. Even if men despoil that wilderness and bring their violence into it, along with their sin and despair, it can still offer to those who look at it a different perspective, the vision of a different world, and the possibility of a God who is bigger than all that is painful and dark. If such power and ruggedness can soften the hard edges of the human spirit, then there is hope that the God who made the wilderness can also remake and renew the rough and tumble of a man's heart.

Mike would never talk to me again. But he was never the tough guy again either. Across the years and the decades, I pray God used the wild country his brother and he loved to take him to a new place in his heart and his life—a place of peace, a place of promise, a place where he and its Maker met and became friends.

24

The Fast River

> He cutteth out rivers among the rocks; and his
> eye seeth every precious thing.
>
> Job 28:10 KJV

There is strength and beauty in the wilderness, experienced
in moments of quiet and solitude. And then there is a different sort of strength and beauty, raw and untamed, when
attempting to engage wilderness in more extreme endeavors.

I was in graduate school, 27, still single, and had just finished presenting a difficult paper on Puritan theology to the
master Puritan himself, J. I. Packer, well known for his work
on the ESV translation of the Bible and for his book *Knowing
God*. Feeling more reckless than usual, I had actually come to
the seminar dressed in a Puritan outfit from head to toe and
played the role of Puritan theologian John Owen throughout
my presentation. Having survived that without any sort of
academic beheading, I was more than ready to disappear

for three or four days and take another risk—canoeing the fast water of the Fraser River in British Columbia, Canada, a pristine waterway that carves its way through hundreds of miles of Canadian wilderness.

There were four of us—Ben, Stan, Lupe, and me—two for each eighteen-foot canoe. It was totally a guy thing—sleeping bags, no tent, hard dry salami, crusty bread, cheese, and apples for food, water for drink. The night before we set the canoes in the water, we all bedded down in the house of Ben's parents. Glancing at the TV guide, I was startled and amused to find an oldie called *River of No Return* on channel 7. Starring Robert Mitchum and Marilyn Monroe, the movie was about three people traveling a dangerous river on a raft, risking their lives. I held up the listing to the others.

"Hey," I said, "what are the odds of a film like this being on TV the night before we head down the Fraser? Maybe God's trying to tell us something."

They laughed and Stan nodded at a newspaper in his hands. "We were just looking over this article in today's paper. It's about canoeing the Fraser."

I was surprised. "Really?"

"Yeah. Listen to this. The guy asks the RCMP where the safest place on the river is to launch their canoes. The cop tells him, 'There is no safe place.'"

Stan grinned and I took the paper from him and read it for myself.

"It says here there are whirlpools and rapids," I told him.

He shrugged. "You knew that."

"Yeah, but this guy says there are real whirlpools and rapids. Not just little things off to the sides by the riverbanks."

Stan yawned. "You'll be fine. Just keep your strokes firm and deep."

"Did you bring the life jackets?"

"Sure." Stan thumped his pillow with a fist and stretched himself out on the couch. "But don't worry about it. Are we not men?"

The four of us hauled the canoes to the river in a pickup and put them in the water just after six the next morning. The sky was clear and we could see detail on both banks long before the sun was up. It was October and the weather was mild. No rain, no hard frost. Light ignited trees turning orange and yellow and red as we slipped past. Smoke from the chimneys of unseen cottages and cabins sometimes drifted over our bows and left the good scent of burning poplar, maple, and elm in our nostrils.

After an hour or two there was no need to paddle. The current was strong enough to pull the wood and canvas canoes forward at a speed we could not match or improve upon, so we sat back and watched the land go by. Red-tailed hawks and bald eagles flew overhead as the blue sky glowed more and more brightly with the ascent of the sun. Ospreys dove and pierced the Fraser in sudden sprays of whitewater. Mule deer drank and watched us cautiously as we appeared and disappeared, their large ears twitching forward and backward.

The canoes were moving so fast in the water the bows hissed. Thousands of small bubbles trailed alongside, gurgling just like ginger ale being poured into a tall glass. It went like this all day. I had never experienced anything like it. Invisible forces propelled our two canoes through the wilderness while we sat back and watched forests and fields and wildlife go about their daily business of being God's creation. I recall Stan smoked a pipe, leaning back, totally relaxed, one hand on the pipe bowl, the other on his knee. Not a care in the world, certainly not the care of paddling a canoe hour after hour. For that matter, we were all totally laid back, the sun golden across our faces and hands, hands empty of the wooden shafts of paddles, no strain, no exertion, no stress. It was a dream day.

As the sun set, the horizon and hills were the color of a ripe peach, and the sandbar where we beached our canoes, a strip of copper. We lit a small fire on the sand and cooked our Genoa salami with sharpened willow branches. The canoes were up well past the high water mark, and we unrolled our sleeping bags even farther back. But the river's voice seemed to be at arm's length as we lay looking up at the soft stars of a warm autumn. I kept drifting in and out of sleep as the river slipped by, murmuring and bubbling.

"Now remember," Stan said, bringing me out of a blue and silver dream. "There's a reason we never had to paddle today. The Fraser is moving fast because something is making it move fast. It's coming out of the mountains north of us, on its way to the sea, flowing faster and faster downhill. There are going to be rapids. You didn't paddle today. You will tomorrow. And you're going to have to paddle hard."

"How hard?" asked Lupe, the youngest one of us.

Stan rose up on one elbow. "Was it a good day, Lupe?"

"Sure."

"Glad you joined us?"

"Yes."

Stan lay back. "Today is worth tomorrow. And tomorrow will be worth it even if there hadn't been today."

"What are you talking about?" I could imagine Lupe screwing his face up in the darkness and I smiled.

Stan did not respond. Only the river spoke, on and on, all night, carrying the stars south on its back, bringing to all who listened thought patterns of the things that mattered most, of life's miles and the distances covered. Massive gray trees, stranded by high water on the Fraser fifty or a hundred years before, loomed large in the dark on the sandbar and riverbank. Exposed roots twisted and turned as if they were still alive, seeking water and food. Night on the river was an unknown world, an alien world, but not really an unfriendly world.

It was a bit of a risk sleeping out in the open. Rain clouds could move in at any time and a downpour soak us to the skin. But it was worth the risk, a small risk, to fall asleep hearing the river clearly and unmistakably, to count the stars, to stare at the tree trunks and gnarled branches. Going out on a fast river was a risk too. And from the sounds of it, the morning would bring a greater risk. But the risk taken had been the dream day gained—coasting on the waters as if we had sails up, eagles in our eyes as we sped south without effort, light crackling on the ripples and bubbles, trees turning to gold right in front of us.

We take risks on God's words and promises, risks others would say are not risks in God's eyes, but steps of faith, yet which seem like risks to us at the time. Some are small—gathering with others on a Sunday morning instead of grabbing two more hours of rest, hoping it will be worth it. Some are large—selling our businesses and becoming pastors, going back to school in our thirties or forties because we sense from God it is the right thing to do, packing up our young families and going to the inner city to work with a church plant or halfway across the world to minister to the poor and starving in India.

When we read the stories of others who have taken the big risks in Christ, we are often startled by the things they have seen, by the things God has done in their lives, things we have never seen nor experienced ourselves. But then, we remind ourselves, we have never put ourselves out on a limb in our commitment to Christ. We have never risked losing the normalcy of our daily existence to gain the astonishing experience of having to see God come through or die. So we have never seen what those who have risked it all on God have seen because we have made sure we have never needed God as much as they have.

Risking the Fraser had provided us the ease and wonder of a day gliding through the wilderness without paddle stroke, as if we rode on air. As we pushed our canoes back into the current in a ruby dawn, we took the bigger risk of facing a big river made more fierce by the surge of waters coming from higher up the mountains. Would it be worth it? Or would we end the day with shattered canoes and cracked bones, wishing we had never been so foolhardy as to launch ourselves onto this river of no return? Who knew? We prayed as we dipped our paddles into the waters.

This stretch of the Fraser was no Class V, and it was not the churning, foaming constriction of the Fraser north of us at Boston Bar that explorer Simon Fraser called the "gate of hell" in 1808. Yet it had teeth and fangs all its own. Our canoes moved without paddling, just as they had the day before, faster and faster, until a new sound hit us—roaring. Roaring that gained in strength and volume as we raced toward it. We rounded a bend and whitewater spread out before us in a riot of waves and foam and leaping water.

"Head into the Vs between the rocks!" shouted Stan, and that was the last I heard from him as he and Lupe and their canoe surged forward into the exploding river.

I had no time to watch their backs. Ben and I had troubles of our own. I was in the bow so it was my job to make sure I stroked the canoe away from last-second rocks and into the Vs of water between them. Ben steered from the stern. Slipping through the rocks was one thing. Taking on waves that smacked together higher than the sides of our canoe was a different matter. I had never run waves thrown up that high before, nor had I ever navigated what opened up just beyond those waves in a swirl of logs and gray water and darkness—a massive grinding whirlpool.

Fear slammed into me with the force of the waves. No matter what we did, the spinning circle pulled us into its mouth. I felt helpless. It would suck us in and break us to pieces in a matter of moments. Our canoe moved with incredible speed into the pit.

Ben was the calmest of all of us, the one least given to sentences with exclamation points. Even now he kept his cool, yet a certain strain came into his voice as he spoke two words: "Paddle, Mur." They were not said in a loud voice. But he packed more urgency into those three syllables than I had ever heard from him before. This was it! We paddled or else.

Hearing stress in Ben's voice was something new. It made me dig deep into the waves and foam. I doubt I ever struck water harder or put my paddle into a river with more drive and intensity. We went at it like madmen. I glanced to my right and saw the whirlpool's dead eye and the edge of its lip where descent began. We dug and dug as if the Fraser were earth and we were making every effort to turn it over and over.

We came flying out into flat calm below the rapids. Stan and Lupe were a hundred feet ahead. In a moment of exuberant relief and adrenalized joy, Ben and I held the paddles over our heads with both hands and shouted in victory. Stan and Lupe lifted their paddles in response and hollered back. Our cries hammered back and forth from one side of the river to the other. But as sweet as overcoming this challenge was, a greater prize, totally unexpected, was just around another curve in the river's flow.

The river broadened considerably after the whirlpool and the current slowed to what felt like a standstill. It was like paddling into a large pond or a small lake. Sun gleamed over the calm surface as we moved silently through wild geese. There were hundreds of them and perhaps as many as a thousand. Resting, undoubtedly, on their way south. Stretching from bank to bank and far ahead, floating, turning now and then with a gentle kick of their feet, serene, at peace, letting us slip between them as if we too were nothing more than slightly larger versions of them. The Canada goose in gray, white, and black majesty.

This was yet another wonder in a day of wonders. This was a moment of peace willingly received after a moment of danger. If we had stayed at home and decided against the trip, and if we had decided whatever good we might experience did not outweigh the risks, we would have missed this moment of grace. We paddled among the geese for ten or fifteen minutes, as if we were making our way among lily pads that had blossomed with an unusual and rare beauty.

Then they began to talk, and the talk became a roar, and the roar became the unfolding of their wings and their rise to the blue heavens, enough to block out the sun, body upon body, crying a cry as wild as the wail of the loon or the howl of the coyote or the bugling of the elk. They flew and our hearts were stung with the strong glory of a magnificent creation.

What do we miss by not taking risks when God speaks to our hearts? What do we lose? Gaining a few more days and years of normal life, we lose our souls and the adventure of life lived to the full, the kind of life Jesus wants to give us.

"I have come that they may have life, and have it to the full" (John 10:10).

The risks may seem great, but the rewards are greater. And though we call them risks, we also call them acts of faith—faith in God and what he can do in and through us. Despite our fears, launching out into an unknown where God invites us and calls us does not diminish our manhood or life span.

On the contrary, responding in such a fashion expands the man in us, as well as the quality and depth of our lives and our souls. Without faith, there is no life. Acting in faith, we go where we have never been before and we live forever.

It is the wilderness we enter by foot or water or air that teaches us to do this. We leave much behind and enter the wild places with the bare necessities. But we return with more than enough, inside and out.

> Everybody needs beauty as well as bread, places to play in and pray in, where Nature may heal and cheer and give strength to body and soul.[1]

John Muir

---

1. John Muir, *The Yosemite* (New York: The Century Company, 1912), 256.

25

Davy Crockett's Rifle

This is what the Lord says: "Stand at the cross-roads and look; ask for the ancient paths, ask where the good way is, and walk in it, and you will find rest for your souls."

Jeremiah 6:16

Set up road signs; put up guideposts. Take note of the highway, the road that you take.

Jeremiah 31:21

We live in a world where things happen fast, and often the work we do is expected to have a quick turnaround with almost immediate results. Yet God does not always work in the instant mode. There are times when he does what he does in a slow, measured rhythm. If we are not patient enough to let him do it that way then we lose the depth and maturity and wisdom God wants to develop in our lives.

Davy Crockett had a .40-caliber Pennsylvania rifle, "Old Betsy," a gift from his constituents to honor his service in the Tennessee State Assembly. He claimed to have shot and killed 125 bears with it. The rifle never went to Texas with him in 1835, but it's at the Alamo Museum in San Antonio just the same. He didn't take "Pretty Betsy" with him either, a rifle presented to him by the Whigs of Philadelphia. Whatever rifle he used at the Alamo, actual reports from Mexican officers at the siege describe a tall, slender man in fringed clothing with an animal fur hat whose shooting was deadly accurate at ranges from 100 to 250 yards.

The fact that Crockett left behind his beloved .40-caliber flintlock that had harvested so many bears tells me he knew he needed a bigger caliber for the game of the western frontier of 1835 and 1836. Historians feel pretty certain some of Jacob Dickert's rifles were at the Alamo, and it's a good bet Crockett had one of them. Dickert crafted his rifles at his home in Lancaster County, Pennsylvania, but they were often sold at supply houses in St. Louis and New Orleans to outfit travelers heading toward the Rocky Mountains or the great Texas plains. These Dickert firearms were .50 caliber or better to suit the hunting of buffalo, grizzly bears, and elk. A number of experts believe Crockett likely had a .54 caliber Dickert at the Alamo, and this conjecture sits well with me. I was born in 1954 and when I turned to black powder shooting, .54 was the caliber I wanted.

It was an Episcopalian priest who showed me the ways of black powder shooting, a man who loved to work on fine shotguns, and for that reason I forever after referred to him as Black John instead of Father John. Black powder or muzzle loading was something I had wanted to get into for years. It thrilled me to think I could actually own and fire a rifle like Crockett and Boone had carried into the raw American wilderness of the 1700s and 1800s.

The movie *Jeremiah Johnson* had a huge impact when it came to black powder. I watched it on the big screen when I was still a teen. I dreamed of going into the Canadian Rockies and building a log cabin and living off the land. Many of my friends had the same vision. We wrote letters asking if homesteading was possible—did the government still give out 160-acre plots you could earn the title to if you cleared a certain amount of land each year? (They didn't—the last homesteading had been offered in the 1950s.)

Then there were all the Fess Parker Crockett shows I'd grown up with. Nothing made me happier than to watch Disney bring up the Frontier Land icon at the start of a Sunday night show. When the day came that I could purchase a firearm, I went out and got a Winchester 94 and spent the evening working the lever in my bedroom. It wasn't Davy Crockett's rifle, but at least the design harkened back to the late 1800s and there was certainly merit in that.

Once Black John introduced me to black powder shooting, I joined the local club and started attending gatherings that imitated the mountain man or free trapper rendezvous. Toting a replica of the famous Hawken rifles made by Jacob and Samuel Hawken, I shot at gongs and candle flames and strings. I blazed away at playing cards set with their edges toward me. I also trained myself to hold the heavy barrel straight and steady long enough to send a round ball accurately into a target. I threw tomahawks and knives. I crafted a possibles bag out of cowhide, and learned to use a powder horn and powder measure.

Suddenly a new hunting season was opened up to me, a season available only to black powder shooters and archers with long bows or recurves (the kind without wheels and pulleys that curved back on themselves at their tips). This was *Last of the Mohicans* stuff—I had to tread more softly and get closer to game than I ever had before. Crockett and Boone may have been able to nail deer at 250 yards, but I wasn't going to try anything like that with iron sights. One hundred or less was my comfort zone. This was an unusual type of hunting that couldn't be done from a distance.

Years later I still did not have what I considered a Crockett rifle though. I had it in my mind that it needed to be .54 caliber with a browned barrel 45 or 46 inches long. The stock had to be carved from curly or tiger maple. And it needed to be a flintlock—even though the percussion cap had been around for a few years when Crockett made his final stand at the Alamo, I was pretty sure he would stick with something that had worked for him all of his life. After fruitless searching locally, as well as calling the regular stores, I finally took the bit in my teeth and called Dixie Gun Works in Union City, Tennessee. They patched me through to Turner E. Kirkland.

Turner was still president of the company he had founded. With his easy southern drawl and a smile that came right through the phone line, he asked me a few questions about what I was looking for. We had a good back and forth, and he pulled a rifle off a rack in front of him. Custom made, no patch box, just wood from stock to muzzle. Once the rifle was in my hands (after a couple of weeks' wait for the Pony Express to make it from Tennessee to British Columbia), I immediately christened it "Tiger." The stripes ran dark and deep over the smooth golden wood, and I felt like kissing it. Maybe I did. It was the best looking rifle I'd ever owned in my life, even beating out the wood on a high-end Weatherby that had once been in my gun safe.

With the target shooting and the black powder rendezvous get-togethers and the early season primitive hunt, God brought a certain amount of relaxation into my life. You can't hurry a flintlock, and you have to concentrate and hold her dead steady between the flash in the pan and the main ignition in the barrel. Soon enough some of the guys started using modern muzzleloaders for their early hunts, inline black powder rifles with stainless barrels and fiberglass stocks, and I can't say they didn't have their own kind of good looks, but for me the challenge always was to hunt and shoot like Crockett and Boone had. And in the end, that is how God saved me.

We all have our different ways of dealing with stress. We don't want it to turn us into angry men who are always spitting out harsh words and slamming truck doors. So we strive to get rid of it. Long hikes with the dogs or weight lifting usually takes the venom out of me. Prayer in a forest or by a stream helps drain it off too. Yet one green January on Vancouver Island, nothing seemed to be working.

It was a church thing. I was the pastor, someone was upset about something or other, and they were working hard to split the church over it. My stomach was tight as new rope and it churned like whitewater. I couldn't sleep. I couldn't eat. Couldn't smile. Could hardly pray.

It was so bad I was actually thinking about giving the whole mess one more shot and then packing it in. A friend had left his church and pastoral ministry under similar circumstances not long before. Maybe that was the way I should be heading. Sometimes a man needs to make a fresh start somewhere else. Perhaps even a pastor needs to put his hands firmly onto another plow. One morning I picked "Tiger" off the rack and disappeared to the shooting range.

The black powder club did not have a regular kind of range. It was carved out of thick forest, and the longest shot you could take was 100 yards. No one else was there when I showed up. I immediately began to load and fire, and I did it all day.

The loading and firing sequence is the only thing on your mind. Tip the large Cureton horn, measure the charge of 2F or 3F black powder, pour it down the barrel, put patch and ball on the muzzle, take the ramrod and push them down onto the charge, tip the small Cureton horn, prime the pan with fine 4F powder, cock the flint, lift the rifle, hold it steady, squeeze the trigger, keep holding steady while the flint shaves hot metal onto the priming, ignites it, shoots flame through a channel into the barrel, makes the main charge explode, and hurls the lead ball forward until there is the smack of the ball hitting target and wood.

You do this again and again to fire only half a dozen rounds. Unless you're in a race or battling off marauders, you take your time. This is quite different from chambering a round into a bolt-action Remington or a lever-action Marlin and completely different from firing a semiautomatic. The weapons of the modern era move swiftly. Those of the 1700s and early 1800s make you go at it more methodically.

The first day of shooting stopped the churning inside a bit, but not enough. I had more time off coming to me, so I used it and drove out to the range a second day. I went through the same ritual of loading and firing and blowing down the barrel to get rid of sparks. My lips were black. The rhythm, the cool winter air, a sky gray and blue, a breeze that came and went—all the slow and natural things worked on me. Load and fire, load and fire, smoke hanging over my shoulders and amongst the tree branches. Soon there was nothing else inside my head except the rhythm and, eventually, God's presence. The churning and tightness and anger were gone. I could return to my congregation and handle the problems there in prayer and peace. The church did not split and the person who had wanted to split it laid down his sword.

There are old paths God takes us down and old ways he uses which the modern world discarded long ago. Even churches have discarded them. There are old teachings in God's Word that have been discarded along with the ancient pathways, teachings no one teaches anymore, passages no one cares to remember or consult. Yet these old things are the very things people need. The new and faster highways with their slick and ultramodern teaching are not getting them where they need to go. Because where they need to go is not a place but a work of God—the careful work he does inside them. When we move too fast it actually slows what God wants to develop and shape and bring to maturity in us in order that we may live well.

I needed Davy Crockett's rifle that week in January. God knew what I needed years before that week arrived. An M16 wouldn't have done it for me, not even my beloved Remington Sendero "Pale Rider." I needed the long, slow, ancient way of shooting to deal with my stressed-out body and tensed-up soul, just like many of us need God's long, slow, ancient way of healing a mind or feeding a spirit with words tried and proven over the centuries.

Our Bible reading can be fast, our prayers even faster, our lives faster yet. God has ways of slowing us down and making us new, ways like wilderness camps and high mountain climbs, and even ways like black powder rifles, and he will make use of any or all of them to put heart in us once again. We just have to be willing to take an older path that others have let grow over with thorns and weed and neglect, a path God blazed by his Spirit and which remains under his eagle eye and protection. We need the ancient forests and the ancient mountains and streams, the good ways, whether they are the places of nature and creation we enter with rod or camera or muzzleloader in hand, or the spiritual places within our souls we enter with prayer and worship and questions. In these present times, we need those ancient pathways badly.

26

The Bird Dog
Who Had Other Ideas

Mortals make elaborate plans, but God has the
last word.

Proverbs 16:1 THE MESSAGE

We always have plans for our children, family members, and
friends. And for our own lives. Sometimes things work out
just as we hoped they would. Other times, life goes in a totally
different direction from what we had planned or expected.

One of our dogs, Nahanni, almost got named Spitfire. Not
because she had a nasty temperament, but because she had
boundless energy and always wanted her own way. She was
unstoppable. And if there was nothing better to do, pouncing
on her brother Yukon and initiating a wrestling match was
much better than boredom. Few things gave her more excitement than playing hide-and-seek with the family members
of her pack—she would yip and squeal as she came on at

full speed, tracking with her nose, always finding us behind a tree or building, then leaping on Yukon for another fight in her sheer happiness at being alive.

It became apparent as I walked her on Vancouver Island that she had a talent for sniffing out and flushing ruffed grouse. They could never hide from her. The trouble was she was never content to root them out of their holes and step back. She always seemed to take exception to the way they ran and how they flapped their wings and the squawks they made. An annoyed look crossed her face and she lit out after them, never biting or catching one, but keeping them going at full speed until I called her back. She had the potential of being a good grouse dog if I could stop her from chasing them out of sight.

So I took Nahanni to a man who trained bird dogs and asked him to make her a grouse, ptarmigan, and quail hunter. He worked with her two evenings a week for a couple of months. I'd ask how she was coming along and he'd laugh in a good-natured way.

"Well, we'll see, we'll see," he'd say.

I asked if she'd make a prime grouse dog.

"She does have it in for those birds, don't she?" was how he answered my question.

"What do you mean?" I responded. "She's smart enough, isn't she?"

"Oh, she's plenty smart, got both Lab and coyote in her, didn't you say?"

"Yes."

"And she's fast. Quick reactions. Great nose. Haven't been able to fool her yet."

"So she'll make a topnotch bird dog?"

He smiled. "She does have it in for those grouse."

I had dreams of Nahanni flushing grouse and other game birds, visions of her swimming out into marshes and fetching mallards and geese I'd harvested with my shotgun. She'd stand perfectly still beside me, sharp ears up, eyes big, body trembling, waiting for my command to go for a downed duck. When I gave the word, and only then, she'd plunge into the water with a coyote yip and paddle like an otter. The same with grouse: I'd give the command, she'd track them down and flush them into the open, then I'd give another command and she'd fly back to my side while I aimed my firearm at the running birds. That was the plan.

Finally she was ready, and just in time for a fall grouse hunt.

"All done?" I asked the trainer.

"Well, we'll see, we'll see."

"Is she going to be okay out in the field?"

"Go for a hunt. See how she performs. Let me know if you pick up on any problems."

"Do you think there are going to be problems?" I pushed him.

He laughed. "She has it in for those birds, no mistake."

We left an unhappy Yukon at home and drove up to some empty logging roads in the Cherokee. Nahanni sprang out and began to examine the dirt track with her eyes and nose. No doubt she picked up on black bear and cougar and deer, maybe even wolf. But I wanted her focused on grouse.

"Birds," I told her. "Birds."

If I'd used the word "fish" she'd have headed for the nearest stream—her grasp of vocabulary was growing by leaps and bounds. But at the tone, inflection, vowels, and consonants of the spoken word "birds" she immediately dropped her head and began to root around in the brush at the edge of the road. Fallen trees with enormous old trunks were the grouse's specialty and hers. In five minutes she had two of them on the run through the short grass.

"Back!" I ordered, swinging my arm backward. "Nahanni! Back!"

For a split second she thought about it. "Back" was the command she'd been trained to respond to. She almost returned to my side. Then a sharp look of annoyance passed over her face. She made up her mind and tore after the birds, yipping and snapping. They ran ever harder. I had raised my shotgun, but it was impossible to get off a decent shot. Nahanni was right on top of them, furious. I shouted at her several times before she finally broke off her attack.

I scolded her. "Nahanni! You are supposed to come! Bad dog! Bad!"

She lowered her ears and slunk to me, looking fearful and sad.

"Okay," I said, "we'll try again."

The two of us walked along the logging road. Ten minutes later she leaped behind a log and chased three ruffed grouse out of hiding. They fluttered up and began to hotfoot it down the side of the road. Perfect. I raised my shotgun.

"Back!" I called. "Back!"

I might as well have been shouting at the moon. Nahanni glared at the retreating grouse, seemed greatly irritated at their squawking and lifting of wings, barked once, and scrambled after them. Dust and feathers flew. Just like the other times, she never caught one or injured one, but she sure got them out of sight and out of range faster than a speeding bullet. Or pellet. I lowered my shotgun. Once again she was too close to the grouse for me to risk squeezing the trigger.

Back to the trainer we went.

"It may never work out the way you want," he warned me. "Grouse infuriate her. I don't believe she can ever keep herself from lighting out after them, no matter what the rewards and punishments are. It's something in her blood."

"You said she was smart and fast and had a good nose," I reminded him.

"She does."

"Please keep trying."

He spent another four sessions with her.

"Well?" I asked when the final session was done.

"Well," he replied, "we'll see."

Nahanni and I were up early the next morning and out to our favorite logging road. The hunt began and she was soon nose down, rustling among the bushes and trees. An explosion of wings and feathers brought up my shotgun, finger on the trigger guard.

"Back, Nahanni!" I shouted, swinging my left arm vigorously. "Back!"

She hesitated longer than she had ever hesitated before. Then a gleam came into her eyes and a dark look crept over her face. If she'd had eyebrows they would have slashed downward. It was clearly more important that the ruffed grouse of the planet be put in their place than she race back to my side. This was something she knew I did not understand, but with time and the proper training I might one day understand and thank her. Risking my wrath, she slipped into high gear and pelted along the roadway after her prey.

Once again, she neither caught nor bit any of them. But she was successful in scattering them to the four winds and at a speed it's likely the grouse never knew they were capable of reaching. I lowered my Browning—as before, no shot was possible without the likelihood of hitting her. Mission accomplished, she slunk back to me, ears flat against her head. I said nothing. We made our way to the Cherokee.

"I don't know what to do," I complained to the trainer a few days later.

"Just let her be," he replied.

"But she has the brains and speed to be a great bird dog!" I protested.

"She does. But it doesn't appear to be her calling in life. I tell you what she will be—a great companion to you and your wife, and when the kids come along, she will be absolutely perfect with them. She'll help you raise your daughters and sons and you'll never have to worry about her hurting them. I guarantee that."

He was right. Nahanni was six when my son was born and eight when my daughter came into the world. She guarded them, licked them, played with them, and never harmed a hair on their heads, coyote blood or no coyote blood. We have video of her settling down next to them as babies when we spread a blanket on the summer lawn. No one touched the kids without her permission. They were her puppies and they stayed her puppies until she left them when Micah was nine and Micaela seven. She remained a great dog to go into the woods with, and everything in the big wide world interested her. As for hunting ruffed grouse, I did it alone and got enough for a few meals and one or two great tail feather fans.

I had my plans. Nahanni had other plans. She had something else built into her that no amount of training could quell. I might have gone through our fifteen years together always ruing the fact that we were not able to form a hunting team. But eventually I let that dream go and enjoyed a new one—a spirited Lab coyote dog who was loyal to our family and gentle to our children. It all turned out well.

It makes me think of a girl from one of our church families, Kate, who thought she'd be good in law enforcement, was sure God was calling her to be a police officer, but suddenly changed her mind. Then her parents wanted her in university—she tried it once, dropped out, tried it again with a different major, dropped out a second time. The other daughter went through university and got her degree, no problem. Kate, however, was at a loss about what she was going to do. She was smart, quick, and outgoing, but she could not stick to anything her parents had planned for her or she had planned for herself.

Out of the blue she began working at a retail outfit. In no time at all she had a management position. In another year or two she was handed the reins to the whole store and was doing a fabulous job. Who knew?

It's human nature to make plans. It's also human nature to try and stubbornly force those plans when it is apparent that they weren't meant to be. It's like trying to make big knives fit into small scabbards or the wrong guns fit into holsters that were never meant for that make or model—you wind up tarnishing and scratching the knife or gun and damaging the scabbard or holster. I could have kept pushing Nahanni, berating her every time she failed to live up to my expectations, and ruined any man-dog relationship we might have enjoyed. Kate's parents could have nagged and insisted and argued until they were alienated from their daughter. Instead, in both instances, good plans were laid down for better plans that were not arranged or anticipated by the ones doing the planning.

We are bound to have plans and some of them, perhaps many of them, work out pretty close to what we want and what we have prayed for. But other times, like a small breeze in a big forest, we need to listen for God's whisper just as Elijah did in his cave in the desert, so that we can find out what we really need to do when all our own plans have fallen apart (1 Kings 19). Sometimes, like when Paul tried to get the gospel into Asia, failing again and again, we have to set aside our own dreams for God's better ones (Acts 16). When we learn to line ourselves up with God's plans and dreams for us and those we love, moments of sustained frustration and anger diminish, while hope, satisfaction, and peace flourish. "Pray that the Lord your God will tell us where we should go and what we should do" (Jeremiah 42:3).

27

Wild Geese

And God said, Let the waters bring forth abundantly the moving creature that hath life, and fowl that may fly above the earth in the open firmament of heaven.

Genesis 1:20 KJV

But ask now the beasts, and they shall teach thee; and the fowls of the air, and they shall tell thee.

Job 12:7 KJV

There are few sights in the autumn sky that put more strength and heart into a person than to see hundreds of wild geese heading south in a ragged V. Their long lines and haunting calls evoke the spirit and power of the wilderness in the same way the wolf's howl can, or the loon's strange cry, or the bull elk's screech and roar. While geese are great hunting and great eating, sometimes the beauty is not in the eating, but in the seeing. My first memory of eating wild goose includes biting into buckshot. I almost broke my teeth. The meat was excellent, but sometimes the small pellets of birdshot escape the notice of even the most scrupulous cook. The Canada goose makes for fine eating, and there's many a sportsman and his family who enjoy it more than a grain-fed turkey at Thanksgiving or Christmas.

During the winter, many lakes remain unfrozen where I live, so few of the geese in our region migrate south. Strong winds from the Pacific break up the ice on lakes and ponds and reservoirs. We do see the ragged Vs moving back and forth over the sky crying their cry, but they are moving from one lake or stretch of water to another. I have seen an eighty-foot bend of the Oldman River crammed with hundreds and hundreds of Canada geese, happy and content and murmuring among themselves in the middle of January. So it was not a strange occurrence to park my Cherokee at an open field near a reservoir and see dozens of geese walk away rapidly, then lift up into the sky, honking. However, it was strange that one goose did not move at all, even though it was clearly alive.

I did not notice the goose until I saw the dogs scampering around him, tails wagging, wanting him to play. I chased them off and approached. He was having trouble walking, could not fly, and was terrified as I squatted next to him. I spoke quietly and guarded myself against a strike from his bill and strong neck, but there was no aggression in him. He was exhausted.

I couldn't see any wounds on his body. Gently, I lifted each wing, all the time continuing to talk in a low, nonthreatening voice. His right wing had blood underneath. Not from buckshot, not even from teeth or claws. Perhaps he had struck or been struck by another goose. It might have happened against a boulder or stump. There was not a large amount of blood, and whatever flow there had been had stopped.

It was not hunting season. It was not time to harvest a goose. But it might be time to set one free. Although his wing was hurt, there was a good chance it might heal. His webbed feet were undamaged. He was having trouble moving about on land, but he might not have the same trouble on water. In any case, if he stayed on shore he was a meal for the coyote or fox. So I picked him up to carry him to the lake.

He was heavier than I expected—the Canada goose is a big bird. And soft. His feathers and long neck felt like velvet. I thought that now there might be a struggle or attack, but he only arched his neck so he could look at me. That look, only a few inches from my face, I will never forget. Large and lustrous, his dark eye seemed almost human. He expected death. There is no other way to describe the expression in his eye.

And why wouldn't he anticipate that? Man hunted him for food and so did most other mammals. Mercy would not even be in the goose's vocabulary or any part of his comprehension or instinct. I would kill him. That's all he could look forward to.

I lugged him down to the beach, continuing to talk quietly. The dogs followed, but I ordered them back—the goose had enough fear to deal with. Putting my waterproof boots into the ripples, I waded out ten or twelve feet, carefully placing him in the lake. Surprised to be plopped gently down into one of his elements, he looked about him. I suspect he was trying to see if there were other geese nearby. In fact, there was a gaggle floating a hundred yards away, hugging the shoreline. He began to paddle, moving rapidly away from me.

Scarcely a month later, I was speaking to a crowd of people at a special memorial service for people who had died of cancer. Survivors, loved ones, and those battling various forms of the disease sat in long rows of chairs. Some had received all kinds of emotional and spiritual support, many had not. Cancer had taken my own father. I tried to speak hope and faith into them, very much aware of my own loss as I did so.

There were fighters in front of me who were not receiving the love and support they needed because addiction to tobacco, in the form of cigarettes, cigars, and smokeless tobacco, had given them cancer of the throat, or mouth, or lungs. It was hard to understand why some family members, as well as religious friends, had turned their backs on them in their hour of greatest need just because they had been smokers. All of us have personal problems and issues, and all of us make mistakes, serious mistakes. But where was the mercy? As I spoke, I remembered the Canada goose with the wounded wing.

"When I picked him up to carry him down to the water," I told them, "I could see he thought I was going to kill him. It was in his eyes. Mercy was something he could not understand and had never received. Once I put him in the lake, he swam away in freedom. It strikes me that many of you have not received mercy from those who ought to have surrounded you and upheld you with it. You are alone and afraid. Family has deserted you and religious people have hurt you. But the same God who put it in me to have mercy on a wounded bird, who put it in me to be a good steward of the earth and all the fish and fowl and animals he created, has also put it in me to tell you today that he loves you. He wants to be closer to you, more than ever before, in his Son Jesus Christ, and not farther away. He does not condemn you. He wants to pick you up and carry you to the water and set you free. He wants to have mercy on you."

I don't know if the goose I rescued survived. I don't know how many of the cancer victims I spoke to that day survived.

But I had mercy on one of God's creatures regardless of what it could or could not understand. And God had mercy on those men and women who reached out to touch his love regardless of what they could or could not understand.

In the end, we can't grasp all there is to know about God or his ways or the ways of the world or the universe. We can't comprehend the depths of human suffering and misery or the suffering of the animal kingdom, a kingdom that suffers because of us, just as Jeremiah the prophet groans, "How long must this land mourn? Even the grass in the fields has withered. The wild animals and birds have disappeared because of the evil in the land" (Jeremiah 12:4 NLT).

It is impossible to understand everything. Or fix everything. But anyone can love and show mercy, the same love and mercy God shows, because we are all made in the image of that very God, and if we believe it and want it, that God lives in our hearts.

The sky was clear, with only a few thin gray clouds in the west, when I released the Canada goose into the lake. Skeins of other geese flew overhead, some into the copper of the setting sun, others into the dark of the east, where three or four stars already gleamed. The dogs and I watched him swim toward his companions. The water he cut through like a ship was an oil painting of blues and grays and golds. The beauty of the evening was immense and the sky over us all seemed infinite.

"Some days," I said to myself, "they help us by feeding our families or just by flying and making us feel the strength of creation and its Creator. And other days we help them by setting them free to fly. Men and women may be the stewards of creation, and sometimes we are the hunters, but we're all in this together."

28

Aurora

For with thee is the fountain of life: in thy light
shall we see light.

Psalm 36:9 KJV

It is an old truth, often enough forgotten, that light, especially
light that invigorates the spirit, is more obvious once night
settles in. As Thomas Carlyle wrote, "The eternal stars shine
out again, so soon as it is dark *enough.*"[1]

For me, that was the main reason for our trips to a very
special campground right by the Montana border—night. Of
course, the daytime vistas were nothing short of spectacular since we were right in the middle of the Canadian and
American Rockies. One field was always on fire with mountain flowers, and the backdrop of purple peaks and glaciers
made it seem like a scene out of the Austrian Alps in *The
Sound of Music*. A river as emerald and clear as green glass

1. Thomas Carlyle, *Past and Present* (London: Chapman and Hall, 1896), 251.

flowed slowly past our tents and fire pit, eventually changing personality sharply as it picked up speed and roared over a series of rocks and boulders, suddenly in a hurry to get to Hudson Bay a thousand miles away. Deer, fox, and coyote moved in and out of aspens and glades. Grizzly rumbled down a centuries-old path from Montana that brought them out of the mountains to the berry bushes and trout below.

The first time my wife and I tried to camp at Back River Campground we were turned away by park staff—the campground was closed because a grizzly sow and two cubs were feeding there. When we finally did get in, many hours after being told no, we fried up steaks over a wood fire and seasoned them with wild onion Linda had found growing out in the open. Later, when we had Micah and Micaela and started bringing them to Back River, they were excited and horrified to discover black widow spiders, with their distinctive red hourglass, living up in the corners of the washrooms. That, plus the sight of bald eagles and ospreys and the threat of grizzlies, set the campground apart from the backyard and any other place they had ever pitched their tents.

The four of us tubed the river, enjoying the slow going of the first few miles, whooping when we hit the rapids, bouncing over the rocks, and darting through whitewater. We hiked the bear trail that snaked down from the peaks, our hearts jumping into our throats whenever the dogs' hackles rose and they refused to go any farther because of the scent they had picked up. We used Bowie knives to carve our initials into a tree, as well as cut shavings for kindling from logs stacked by the fire pit. We watched beaver slide back and forth through the jade waters and slap their tails with the splash of a thrown rock when they detected our presence.

There was no potable water at Back River, showers were nonexistent, electricity could not be had at any price, and cell phones did not work. The only modern amenity was flush toilets. This combination made most people move on to other less primitive sites.

If you stayed at Back River it's because you wanted it rugged, smoky, and a bit more dangerous—not much, just a bit. The kids loved having the freedom to wear the larger fixed blades on their belts. An older Blackfoot man once said to Micah, who was armed to the teeth against the wilderness, "Does the mighty warrior have enough knives for fighting and skinning?"

And I can never forget the look on a woman's face as she saw me emerge from the bushes wearing nothing but khaki shorts and a Bowie knife almost as long as her car. I was tanned pretty dark from the sun and might have had a stone dangling from my neck by a leather thong as well. She quickly put the pedal to the floor and squirted out of sight around a bend in the road. I wanted to call to her, "Wait, it's okay, I'm a Baptist pastor!"

The days were supreme, but night was king. The fire roared, food was cooked, dishes cleaned, tales told as the coals flared in the night breeze. Micaela and Micah, running to the washrooms and back with their flashlights, were happily scared by the coughs, snorts, and barks of startled whitetail. Only the fire held the darkness at bay. The black of midnight was absolute. So we ringed the flames and absorbed their heat, drank hot chocolate, and made s'mores.

I never wanted my family to turn in. Yes, it was both comforting and exhilarating to crawl into a warm sleeping bag, lantern by your side, a big knife in its sheath next to your hand, and snuggle down to sleep with only the thin membrane of the tent wall between you and the wilderness. But I argued that the greatest show in the wilderness always began when it was dark enough and not before.

The stars would come out thicker than you could see them in city or town, brighter and more robust than they would ever be at sea level or on the flat prairie. The high elevation and lack of city glare gave the night sky the appearance of millions of jewels strewn over black ermine, glittering with a cold and unearthly fire. Usually I won my argument and we walked away from the orange fire to stand in the grass together and look up at what really was a Milky Way, white stars pouring across our galaxy, so rich and creamy you could hardly see the dark spaces between them. If it was August, there was the added excitement of shooting stars. Only after soaking in such a divine spectacle for a good half an hour or more would I let my wife turn in without further debate. My children might stay with me a bit longer, but I was always the last man standing. Or lying down—sometimes I lay flat on my back on a picnic table, hands behind my head, and watched the thousand suns burn from that vantage point.

It is, as I say, a lesson often learned and often forgotten—no matter how dark the night, the stars are brighter, and even though the stars are there all the time, we cannot see them while the sun shines and life is bright. It takes darkness for us to see the light that is hidden from our eyes. In the same way we think little of God's Spirit and his miracles and power, we scarcely give a thought to his fiery angels, until we really need them, when we are beyond human help, when money cannot buy us peace or joy or security, when our talents and abilities and those of our friends, or those of the best doctors or best lawyers or best pastors, run smack up against our limitations and we are helpless. Then, in our desperation, we see, and often see clearly, God and his angels and his power in our greatest darkness. Perhaps we would not lose hope so quickly if we would recall how brightly the stars of God shine when all light is gone.

Sometimes we are granted an overabundance of light because our need is so great. One night at Back River I had the whole crew standing out under the white pour of the Milky Way when waves of light suddenly overpowered even that. They throbbed scarlet and sapphire and emerald as they covered the sky. Up and down they rose and fell, like vast curtains, dominating the darkness and the lesser lights. Then they turned into circles that ringed the universe that was our sky and the cutout shapes of mountains. Light upon light upon light broke upon us as if the dark roared with rapids and whitewater. It made us feel as if we were something special just by seeing the whirl and swirl and power. It made us feel immortal.

The northern lights. Aurora Borealis. Sometimes they come softly. Sometimes they are a headlong rush of light and color. Sometimes it is only five or ten minutes before they vanish. Other times they crash like breakers over our heads for hours. As sunlight pleases the eyes and heart in one way, and starlight in another, so the Aurora dazzles in ways unlike the others.

The four of us stood transfixed as if God himself were speaking to us. Often his sunlight is enough for our spirits, and in our darkness, his stars. But sometimes nothing less than cascades of light from the heavens will do, light that moves like the wind and sweeps over us like a tsunami. So it was for the shepherds at Bethlehem, who had their own Aurora of angels. So it was for Peter and the others who experienced an Aurora that was the wild burst of Jesus' transformation from merely human to stunningly divine. So it was for the apostles at Pentecost, swept by holy fire, and so it was for John on the island of Patmos, when he turned to see a Christ who had overpowered death and was an Aurora of flame and unending might.

So it may sometimes be for some of us.

29

The Rapids

The river of Kishon swept them away, that ancient
river, the river Kishon. O my soul, thou hast trod-
den down strength.

Judges 5:21 KJV

I had saved Yukon when he was a puppy, lost in the wilderness, and we had enjoyed a great life together. Now, near the
end of his days, I was faced with a heartrending decision to
try to save him a second time, or let him go, and let him die.

The dogs and I were plunging deep into wooded hills and
had taken a deer trail down into a canyon. It was a wonderful
place, cut through with streams and slabs of black rock and
bursting with stands of birch and poplar and wolf willow.
As we explored, Yukon paused to drink from a creek that
ran right through the middle of the canyon, a rush of water
that was bigger than the other streams around us and swollen
to the size of a small river from a weekend of rain showers

and thunderstorms. I scarcely noticed what he was doing, a dog taking a drink in the wilderness being one of the most normal things a dog could do.

Then the current swept in and took his hind legs out from under him. I saw it happen out of the corner of my eye. It was a surprise because I had always been confident my coyote dogs would know what was and was not possible in the wilderness, acutely aware of what they could or could not do. But Yukon was caught off guard and though he paddled to try and get back to shore, it was quickly obvious that this was not going to happen. He was already being pulled into the main current and did not have the strength to get back out.

I ran beside him, calling to him to try harder, to come to me, but he could not do it. A glance ahead showed me where he was going to end up—a waterfall that plunged with a roar onto rocks and boulders below it. Perhaps Yukon would survive the drop. It was not Niagara Falls after all. But the force of the water could hold him under and drown him. His head could strike a rock, breaking his skull in two. A leg could be splintered or ribs smashed in. As I ran, I knew the risk was too great. I could not let him go over the falls.

This was not spring runoff that howled like a demon and churned with massive trees and planks and tore riverbanks apart. But it was cold and fast and angry, and I knew if I jumped in I'd be in for the fight of my life. Yes, I was a father and a husband and I had a family I needed to get home to alive. And yes, there was a difference between saving a human life and an animal life—had it been my son or daughter or wife who had been swept away, I would have already been in the water, doing everything in my power to save them. There would have been no hesitation whatsoever. I was holding back now because I thought Yukon might get back to shore under his own power, that the current might sweep him into an eddy, that I might not have to hazard a leap into the whitewater if everything sorted itself out over the next half minute.

God knows a man often has to do what makes no sense to anyone else. One time, on Vancouver Island, a house fire had quickly turned into an inferno. The fire chief told me that when he arrived on the scene his heart sank like a stone because he knew no one would be alive if they were still trapped in those soaring flames. To his relief, the family was standing together on the street as the first fire trucks arrived.

But a head count showed that the youngest son was missing. He was still in the house. The fire chief saw a look of pain pass between husband and wife. Then the man—the man who was father and husband and who had a wife and two children standing beside him—ran back into the house before the fire fighters could stop him. Shouting out the name of his son, he disappeared into the walls of heat and flame. He never came out. When the blaze was extinguished, they found the body of father and son.

People criticized his decision. He still had a family to live for—how could he be so reckless as to try to rescue a child who was probably already dead? But I knew. The boy could still have been alive, hoping to God his father or mother or a fire fighter would rescue him, screaming in fear. So long as there was that chance, as slim as it might be, the father was going to go in. I knew. Because I was a father and if it had been my son or daughter I would have gone in.

There was no other choice. He had to take the risk to save his son. Or go through the rest of his life agonizing over whether he might have saved his boy and brought him out of the flames. That would be no life for the man. He would be half the person he had ever been. He might have made the difference, but he had been afraid to go in. No, that father had no choice. Those who did not understand were not the fathers of that little boy. Had it been their child, they would have done the same thing that father did.

Life is not a mathematical equation you figure out on a calculator. A man doesn't punch in the numbers and announce, "Oh, I have three left alive, I'll only lose one in the fire, odds are against me getting out with him, so I'll stay here with the others." A father's heart doesn't work that way. Neither does God's.

Remember what Jesus said? That God cares much more for us than the flowers or birds or the rest of creation? That men and women and children are precious to him? That he even knows the number of hairs on our heads? (Luke 12:6–7; Matthew 6:26–30). God the Father sent his Son to save the human race. That is how much we matter to him (John 3:16–17). God does not say, "Oh, it's only one person; they're not worth saving." He gives the life of his Son for every life.

I ran beside the torrent watching the dog that had helped raise my own son and daughter, who had guarded them, had stood between me and bears, had trusted me with his life, get pulled toward a waterfall that might kill him. It was not my son, it was not my daughter or my wife, but it was my companion, it was my friend, and I could not let him die that way. When I saw that nothing was going to save Yukon, I threw myself into the raging water twenty feet ahead.

It felt like a hundred men were kicking and punching me and trying as hard as they could to pull my arms and legs out of their sockets. I was yanked under, but desperately fought my way to the surface. Three times I was pulled under, three times I fought back to the surface, gulping air. Treading water, I struggled to maintain my position as Yukon was swept in my direction. Of course I could not stay in one place, the current was too strong for that, yet I was able to slow down my movement toward the falls by thrashing with my legs and churning with my arms. But the water was cold and fierce, and I was getting tugged down a fourth time.

"GOD! HELP US!"

I roared the words at the top of my lungs and they bounced off the canyon walls. A slipstream caught Yukon up and swept him directly into my arms. I gripped him with one arm and stroked for the shore with the other. I put everything I had into those one-armed strokes, water splashing up and choking me, the current screaming and doing everything in its power to haul me back and over the falls. Mercifully, we found ourselves deposited on a gravel beach and I let Yukon go. He jumped ashore, greeted his distraught mate Nahanni with a lick on the face, shook himself, and carried on, nose to the ground.

I came ashore on all fours, hardly able to get my breath, in an instant feeling all the strain that had been put on my muscles and all the blows the water had inflicted on my shoulders and back and stomach. When I got to my feet, I leaned against a tree. I had felt nothing in the water but the fight. Now I felt like I had tumbled down a mountainside and broken or bruised every bone in my body. My favorite cap had been ripped from my head and was gone forever.

This all happened, oddly enough, on Father's Day. I returned sopping wet to my home and to a table spread in my honor. My wife and young children were eager to surprise me as I stepped through the door. I suppose the way I looked surprised them instead. But after a quick change of clothes I was ready to sit down and celebrate our family and fatherhood with them. All in all it was quite a day.

Some say I shouldn't have rescued Yukon. The risk was too great. I owed it to my wife and children not to jump into that maelstrom of foam and fury. But a man has his own reasons for doing what he feels he must do. No one else could have saved my companion of twelve years. I would be the one who would have to live with his death, a death I might have been able to prevent. I couldn't let him go like that, and I couldn't return to the children who adored him and tell them he had drowned and that there hadn't been anything I could do to save him. There was something I could do to save him. And I did it.

The heart that is in the Father is in us. Not only a heart for humans, as important as they are, but a heart for the animal kingdom too. A righteous man, the Bible tells us, cares for his animals (Proverbs 12:10). When Jonah was furious that God had not destroyed Nineveh, God reminded him, "Nineveh has more than a hundred and twenty thousand people who cannot tell their right hand from their left, and many cattle as well. Should I not be concerned about that great city?" (Jonah 4:11 NIV 1984). In Genesis, God made humans and wild animals and livestock on the same day—and he saw that it was all good, in fact, very good (Genesis 1:24–31).

That is God's heart and the all-encompassing love of the Father's heart. It is the code all God's fathers ought to live by.

30

The Lighter Side of the Mountain

A cheerful heart is good medicine.
Proverbs 17:22 NIV

The wilderness is a place of growth and challenge, discovery and danger. It is also a place where people are free to throw back their heads and laugh with a happiness that reaches to the highest heavens.

I should have known what I was in for when, a few days before our wedding, I was sleeping downstairs in a house full of kith and kin and abruptly wakened by my future wife talking and laughing and clapping her hands in the bedroom just above me. This would not have been so unusual—every man wants a happy wife—except for the fact that Linda had been fast asleep while she did all this.

"Oh, don't worry." They grinned when they saw the look on my face later. "It's just the stress. She'll be fine when the ceremony is over and she's safe and sound in your arms."

I was fast asleep on our wedding night in a honeymoon cabin when Linda screamed. I fell all over the bed looking for the lamp on the table just beside me. When I turned it on my wife's blue eyes were wide with alarm.

"What is it?" I demanded.

"There! Right there!" She pointed wildly across the room. "That thing! That thing on the chair!"

Bewildered, still half asleep, trying to understand what was happening, I looked where she was pointing. A wooden chair stood in the middle of the room and a coat had been thrown across it. Her coat.

I stared at her.

"It's just a coat," I said. "A coat thrown across a chair."

She stared back at me, her eyes still wide. "Who asked you?" she snapped in anger, then flopped her head back on her pillow and promptly fell asleep.

I was left sitting up in bed, wide awake, with my heart pounding, trying to figure her out. Unfortunately, I did not give much thought to what might happen if I transplanted my wife, along with her midnight eccentricities, into the heart of the Canadian wilderness. I soon found out.

We had hiked out to a place called Cape Split that overlooked the Bay of Fundy. There were stories about people falling off the cliff into the roaring tides below. There were even stories about a murderer who would walk with unsuspecting persons to the dropoff and push them over while they stopped to look. This was all fuel for Linda's imagination, of course. That night in our tent I was jolted out of a sound sleep by a sharp whisper.

"The murderer's hand is in the tent. Don't let him know you're here."

The inside of the tent was pitch black. I couldn't see a thing.

"There's nothing," I whispered back.

"Yes, there is. His hand is coming right through the opening. Be quiet and lie still or he'll seize you by the throat."

I did lie still, wondering if she saw something I didn't. One small part of me worried that hard, cold fingers might indeed close around my neck and choke the life out of me. Nothing happened and in the morning she thought I'd made the whole thing up.

A few years later, and after I'd forgotten all about her midnight deliriums (a big mistake), we were camping one night in the Rockies. A soft voice woke me up in the morning as I lay in my bag, head pointing toward the screen door of our two-man tent.

"I wouldn't move if I were you."

Was I in a western? Was my hand, unknown to me, creeping toward a hidden six-shooter, and the guy who had the drop on me noticed?

"What's wrong?" I whispered back.

I had opened my eyes and could see the wide blue eyes in my wife's face. She was staring at something outside the tent door.

"There's a fox," she replied, her eyes too big and too bright. "A big red fox with rabies crouched and ready to spring on your head."

I did not so much as twitch. Foxes could carry rabies and for all I knew a crazed one was crouched outside the tent door ready to make a wild plunge at my throat. I waited several minutes. Linda said nothing more, but continued to stare at the same place. Slowly I turned my head. The ground in front of the tent was empty.

"There's nothing there!" I protested.

"It just left," she said.

Rabid foxes, coats on chairs, and murderers were all grist for Linda's midnight imagination, but living out west, the grizzly bear really caught a hold of her thought patterns. Camping in Tweedsmuir Park in British Columbia one night, we didn't even cook meat, but had a cold meal of apples, cheese, and bread instead, so as not to waft any enticing aromas into the forest. After praying for safety, we snuggled into our mummy bags to await the worst, nightmares or bears—whichever came first. True to form, I was deep into my dreams when fingers dug into my arm like iron nails.

"What is it?" I asked, waking up.

"Shhh!" Even in the dark I could see her eyes. "There are grizzlies outside!"

"Grizzlies!" Fear stung me like a glass of ice water. "How do you know?"

"I can hear them digging a tunnel."

"A tunnel?"

"Yes, they're digging a tunnel under our tent. They're going to get at us from underneath."

That, of course, was when I realized I'd been pulled into one of my wife's nocturnal episodes once again.

I snorted in disgust. "Grizzlies don't dig tunnels!"

"These ones do."

"If they wanted us they'd just tear through the tent with their claws and attack!"

Her anger flared. "Well, now that you've said that, it's probably what they're going to do!"

We survived Tweedsmuir and The Great Tunneling Bears of British Columbia, but *Ursus arctos horribilis* wasn't finished with us, or my wife's active imagination, just yet. Camping in the Rockies of Alberta, in an area known for its large grizzly population, Linda had come up with a plan. If bears showed up, as they were bound to do, she was certain she would be able to handle the fear and pain of a mauling so long as I was holding her hand. If we were attacked in the night, she would take my hand and squeeze it for all she was worth, and this would help her make it through.

"Is it all right if I squeeze your hand really hard?" she asked me.

"Of course," I replied foolishly.

Feeling the chill of the air, I put the hood of the mummy bag over my head, drew the drawstrings tight, and dropped off to sleep. A grip like a steel vice crushed my hand, bringing me to full consciousness.

"Hey!" I said. "What are you doing?"

"Shh!" Linda hissed.

I was annoyed. "Oh, what is it now?" I asked loudly.

Linda got angry. "Shut up!" she whispered harshly. "The grizzlies are just outside the tent and they're trying to get in! I told you I needed to squeeze your hand and I'd be all right! Now they can hear you and they'll come in even faster!"

"How do you know there's grizzlies outside?"

"You can hear them trying to paw through the fabric."

Linda continued to squeeze all blood and life out of my hand as we stopped arguing to listen. A breeze moved through the pines. A night bird chirped once. There was no other noise.

"They're gone," Linda grumbled. "No thanks to you."

"You're sure there were bears?"

"Of course I'm sure!"

"Well, what did it sound like?" I asked her.

"What did what sound like?"

"You said they were trying to get through the wall of the tent. What sound were they making with their paws?"

I felt crazy asking. If grizzlies, or even black bears for that matter, had wanted to get into our tent there wouldn't have been any pawing going on. They would have ripped it open with their teeth or claws in moments. But part of me wondered if maybe bears had been simply rooting around, not wanting to attack us, but trying to scent out food. So I asked.

"Whoosh-whoosh," Linda told me. "Whoosh-whoosh, whoosh-whoosh. That was the sound of their paws scraping against the tent."

"Whoosh-whoosh? Double strokes like that?"

"Yes."

I lay in the dark puzzled. Linda seemed to have heard something, but what? What sort of creature could have made that sound, one stroke on top of the other? And if it hadn't been trying to get into the tent, what had it been trying to do?

Then it hit me. Like a revelation. Perhaps God was having a good time and wanted to finally let us in on the joke too. I grabbed the drawstrings that tightened the hood of my mummy bag.

"Linda," I said. "Listen to this."

I tugged on the strings as I had done earlier when I was cold, first one side, then the other, back and forth, till I had the hood as tight as I wanted on my head.

Whoosh-whoosh. Whoosh-whoosh. Whoosh-whoosh.

If I thought Linda was going to feel relieved and thank me, I was wrong. She slugged me in the arm.

"Oh!" she almost shouted. "You really had me scared! I really did think there were grizzlies trying to break into the tent! You should have told me!"

"What? Woken you up to tell you I was going to tighten the drawstrings of my sleeping bag? You would have loved that!"

She slugged me in the arm again.

My wife is a crack shot with a rifle or handgun, can ride a horse with strong and steady hands on the reins, and is a great RN. The kids love her in Sunday school, my own son and daughter think the world of her, and she has been a great friend and encourager to me in my ministry both as a pastor and a writer. But if you camp out in grizzly country with her, you do so at your own risk. You have to count on losing some sleep and dealing with her midnight adventures on at least one night out of five. Even if she isn't going on about marauding bears in her sleep talk, she'll do it pretty good when she's wide awake too.

However, she has mellowed some over the years we've camped in wild places. Now it's possible for me to lie beside her in our tent in the dark and ask, "Linda, do you know what sound this is?"

Whoosh-whoosh. Whoosh-whoosh. Whoosh-whoosh.

And I don't get a punch in the arm. Instead she laughs and tells me, "It's the sound of a grizzly bear getting into its sleeping bag."

"A happy heart," says God's Word, "makes the face cheerful" (Proverbs 15:13).

31

God's Country

The earth is the Lord's, and everything in it, the
world, and all who live in it.

Psalm 24:1

"The human spirit," wrote an unknown author many years
ago, "needs places where nature has not been rearranged by
the hand of man."

Such places may be hours or days from your home. Or
they may be as close as your backyard. For God is everywhere
and so is the mark of his hand, a hand stronger than ours.

Our children have been fortunate enough to enjoy the
deserts of Nevada and the forests of California, the wild
beaches of Oregon as well as the seascapes of Nova Scotia
and Prince Edward Island, the glaciers of Vancouver Island
and the Rockies of Colorado. But not a half hour from our
door is one of the most wonderful places on earth, Waterton-
Glacier International Peace Park.

This union of Canada's Waterton Lakes National Park and America's Glacier National Park is a World Heritage Site and both parks have been designated as Biosphere Reserves by the United Nations Educational, Scientific and Cultural Organization (UNESCO). Rotary members from Alberta and Montana made the peace park happen and it was dedicated on June 18, 1932. The peace park is also embraced by the Blackfoot Confederacy, whose people make their homes on both sides of the international boundary.

If Waterton-Glacier is sacred ground for the Blackfoot, it is also sacred ground for me. Long before we lived near the park, Linda and I made our way there to camp and hike, even when we had a home on Vancouver Island. I have prayed there, read my Bible under the towering mountain ramparts, raised my children there, and slept with my wife under its moon and stars. When John Muir writes that "going to the woods is going home,"[2] I say amen, especially when it comes to the woods of Waterton and Glacier.

I doubt I have ever taken the park for granted. I know that someday I may live far from its peaks and rivers, so I drive down whenever I get the chance. It can be busy in the summer with tourists pouring back and forth between Montana and Alberta at the Chief Mountain border crossing, yet it is never as crowded and commercialized as its sister mountain park to the north, Banff, or its other sister mountain park to the south, Yellowstone. In a few minutes I can be far removed from sidewalks and restaurants and ice cream cones, finding company amongst elk, eagles, and wolves. It is God's country for me and, as such, holy ground.

But you can still grow comfortable in a place like Waterton-Glacier and expect certain things to happen in one part of it and not another. Bears, for instance, don't usually wander

2. John Muir, "The Forests of the Yosemite Park," *Atlantic Monthly*, April 1900.

into the town. They remain up in the hills and on the mountain trails. Yet it's their land too, so sometimes they show up where they are not expected.

Canada Day is July 1, when Canadians celebrate their nation and its independence in the same way their American cousins do on July 4. It's free to drive into the Waterton area of the peace park that day, and many people take advantage of the gift. A popular hike, mostly in town, starts at the information center and zigzags quickly up a rock face. Called Bear's Hump, it gets you to a beautiful, and often windy, vista where southwestern Alberta and western Montana sprawl to the horizon. Individuals and families, even those with young children, do the hike since it takes little more than half an hour.

As a prelude to everything else we wanted to do in Waterton on Canada Day a few years ago, my family did Bear's Hump. Dozens were streaming up and down the trail. Sometimes we passed others and sometimes others passed us. We got to the top, sat down on the rocks, and enjoyed the view. The weather was in our favor, the wind light, and everyone around us in a celebratory mood. After catching our breath and getting a few pictures, we headed back down. The trail was still crammed with scores of people. Finally we reached a clear stretch and I felt like running.

Running downhill is a lot noisier than walking and my runners, size 15, slammed into the earth at each step. Trees and tall grass grow on both sides of the trail and I had just about reached trail's end, where it hooks to head down to the parking lot, when I approached a cluster of thick bushes. As my feet smacked the ground a big head suddenly burst up from the leaves and branches. I was startled and came to a dead stop. The black bear was only twenty feet away.

He wasn't supposed to be there. Bears rarely come that close to town, let alone graze to the side of one of the busiest trails in the park. Depending on how long he'd been hunkered down in the bush eating, two or three hundred people could have already walked past him, unaware. He obviously couldn't have cared less about all the traffic. It took my big feet and 225-pound body to make him jerk up his head and wonder what the ruckus was about.

In no time he could be on me. I waved to the others to stay back, but my son came racing up anyway because he wanted to see a bear up close. I did not want to risk trying to walk past the bear—I didn't know if he felt threatened or if he was just curious. I didn't want to move backward either. So my son and I stood there and stared at the bear and the bear stared back at us. Surprisingly, the trail had emptied for a few minutes and there were no disturbances above or below.

Seeing a bear when there is nothing between you but a few feet of grass and earth is a different experience from seeing one in a zoo or from inside a car. The fear factor is there, of course, but a strange beauty also surrounds the experience. An untamed creature has wandered down from the crags to lunch on the lush vegetation afforded by the lower slopes. He lives and sleeps in caves. His life revolves around roaming high mountain meadows and eating ants and carrion and berries. My world is utterly different from his.

I want to know more about him. His eyes glisten and so does his fur. We are so close that each black hair is obvious and precise, as if his profile has been meticulously engraved on the air. I sense no hostility from him and he does not sense any from me. We look and look at each other and what do we know about each other? Nothing. Yet I am glad I live on a planet that has regions that are unconquered and animals like him not trapped by excess of roadways or building permits or off-road vehicles. He is still wild and free and I can still see him that way as my son and I stand facing him, and he us.

By now my daughter and wife were at our side. So were others hiking up and down the trail. The bear was showing no aggression, so people hung around and snapped photos and took video. My family did the same. The bear was still great to look at, but with the growing crowd, a bit of the magic was gone. Maybe he felt so too. Five minutes later he dropped his head and was gone. You could see the grass rustling as he made his way along the slope. A few saplings bent to one side. Then it was just the hiking trail and people and cameras. Time for the Puras to push on.

When I use the term "God's country," I mean an area of wild and pristine nature where animals run free and beauty crams the landscape. But the bear came to a place I thought it wasn't supposed to be and made that slope a bigger piece of God's country than it had been before. And the truth is anywhere God shows up is God's country—cities, towns, churches, hospitals, battlefields, protest marches, movie theaters, you name it. And since God is everywhere, that means every place on earth is God's country—"Where can I go from your Spirit? Where can I flee from your presence?" asks the songwriter in Psalm 139:7. And in the book of Jeremiah God challenges Israel, "Do I not fill heaven and earth?" (23:24).

So if God's country is all around us that means all parts of our lives matter to him—work, play, romance, finances, good times, hard times, confusing times—they are all part of his domain. Nothing is left out, everything is under his hand: "If I rise on the wings of the dawn, if I settle on the far side of the sea, even there your hand will guide me, your right hand will hold me fast" (Psalm 139:9–10).

This is a good thing. Consider that the God who made us made the heavens and the earth—the constellations we gaze at from our wilderness camps, the stag and bull elk and pronghorn we photograph and track, the fast river, waterfall, and rocky crag we marvel at, and the bald eagle, red-tailed hawk, and peregrine falcon that make us soar inside as they cut the sky over our heads. If he did all that, and did it so well, what can't he do with our own worlds, our own struggles and defeats and blessings? Why can't he make our own lives God's country if we say yes to his power and greatness and strength? The good news is—he can.

Campfire

The Heart of the World

Thy righteousness is like the great mountains;
thy judgments are a great deep: O Lord, thou
preservest man and beast.

Psalm 36:6 KJV

A man by the name of Hamlin Garland, writing in *McClure's* magazine in February of 1899, confessed, "Whenever the pressure of our complex city life thins my blood and be-numbs my brain, I seek relief in the trail; and when I hear the coyote wailing to the yellow dawn, my cares fall from me—I am happy."

It's a confession all of us who love the wilderness understand and could easily make ourselves. I know that when I consider the stresses and pressures of life and pastoral ministry, I don't know what I would have done without the peace and cleansing and challenge of the wild places. Sure, I did long runs, lifted weights, swam lengths at indoor pools, worshiped, and prayed, but without God's wilderness I wouldn't have made it. Is that so odd a thing? It is we who have built the towns and cities. It is he who built the forests and mountains. Why should anyone think it strange I go there to find him and worship the God of heaven and earth and my salvation?

I know that not everyone wants the smoke of a fire at the end of the trail or the end of a hunt. Not everyone wants to rough it in the mountains or see a bear from twenty feet away. But for those of us who do, God has a rare treat in store—getting to know him in a way that is exciting and unique. Creation was made by God, and it is the Maker of the wilderness that people pray to, not the things made, stunning as they are. As a book by its style and content tells you something about the person who wrote it, or a painting something about the artist, so the wild country tells you something about the God who thought it up and put it together.

> They know the truth about God because he has made it obvious to them. For ever since the world was created, people have seen the earth and sky. Through everything God made, they can clearly see his invisible qualities—his eternal power and divine nature. So they have no excuse for not knowing God.
>
> Romans 1:19–20 NLT

Far from obscuring God and what is in his heart, the wilderness reveals it. Martin Luther knew this: "God writes the gospel, not in the Bible alone, but on trees, and flowers, and clouds, and stars."[1]

So did Shakespeare: "And this our life, exempt from public haunt, finds tongues in trees, books in the running brooks, sermons in stones, and good in everything."[2]

1. Martin Luther, *Watchwords for the Warfare of Life*, trans. Elizabeth Rundle Charles (New York: M. W. Dodd, 1869), 191.
2. William Shakespeare, *As You Like It*, 2.1.15–17.

Elizabeth Barrett Browning knew it too: "Earth's crammed with heaven, and every common bush afire with God."[3]

John Muir never forgot it: "Every particle of rock or water or air has God by its side leading it the way it should go. . . . In God's wildness lies the hope of the world."[4]

And Jeremiah the prophet confirmed it: "It is he who made the earth by his power, who established the world by his wisdom, and by his understanding stretched out the heavens" (Jeremiah 51:15 ESV).

A friend told me that whenever life becomes too much to handle he picks up his rifle and a shaker of salt, crams a New Testament into a jean pocket, and heads into the wild country to pray and sleep under the stars. I may not have always had the rifle and shaker of salt, but I have taken the New Testament, my dogs, and sometimes my family or a close friend, and done much the same thing. The wild air and green spaces clear the head and cleanse the soul. The same may be said of the dry air and brown spaces of the desert. Muir challenged us to "keep close to Nature's heart . . . and break clear away, once in a while, and climb a mountain or spend a week in the woods. Wash your spirit clean."[5]

For we know, or ought to know, that these are places to find Christ again, to know his sacrifice and resurrection in the deeper ways lost in traffic and bills and human turmoil. The wild is one of the best regions to rediscover your faith. As Paul says, Christ is the image of the invisible God and by him everything was created, in heaven and on earth, visible and invisible, all things were made by him and for him, and in him

3. Elizabeth Barrett Browning, "Aurora Leigh" in *The Poems of Elizabeth Barrett Browning* (New York: James Miller, 1874), 275.

4. John Muir, *John of the Mountains: The Unpublished Journals of John Muir* (Madison, WI: The University of Wisconsin Press, 1979), 319, 317.

5. S. Hall Young, *Alaska Days With John Muir* (New York: Fleming H. Revell, 1915), 216–217.

everything holds together (Colossians 1:15–17). Everything . . . and especially creation not rearranged by human hands.

Small wonder, then, that many people will tell you that one of their greatest spiritual experiences occurred in the setting of a Christian camp. Such places are less fettered by human rules and conventions, where God can be more hands-on with us. Church buildings are one place a person can discover God. The wilderness is another. Both are used by him. No building holds God in or lays exclusive claim to his Spirit, and neither does any valley or mountaintop. Solomon admitted this: "The heavens, even the highest heaven, cannot contain you. How much less this temple I have built!" (1 Kings 8:27). God speaks to us wherever he will—a church, a house, a forest, a desert. And God makes his temple in a believer's heart and in the whole world of believers' hearts.

For those who wonder about my love of God's wild, I have pointed out that Jesus got up early and went to quiet and lonely places to spend quality time with the Father—"But Jesus Himself would often slip away to the wilderness and pray" (Luke 5:16 NASB). He prayed on mountainsides (Matt. 14:23) and in desolate, isolated spots (Mark 1:35). Even when he was in a city like Jerusalem, he sought out trees and green and solitude—the Garden of Gethsemane on the Mount of Olives. Tempted in the wilderness, he met angels there, and wild animals, and emerged focused and rejuvenated: "Then Jesus returned to Galilee, filled with the Holy Spirit's power. Reports about him spread quickly through the whole region" (Luke 4:14 NLT). Those who do not want to be in the wild with God prefer him at home or in the pew. And, of course, God will meet them there. But they miss so much by not meeting the Father in the way Jesus often did.

Once, I went into the wild a dead man. Death had broken my heart and I grieved. I had nothing left for wife or family or the church where I pastored. I sat among the trees and read the Bible and gave God my pain and anger and hopelessness. One by one, the stars came out. At dawn, the sun rose clear of the mountains and hills. The birds moved swiftly from branch to branch. Whitetail drank at the green river. I walked with the dogs to a marshland and jumped when a bull moose with a full rack roared and splashed through the water away from us. The sun set in red and purple, the moon came back with the stars, fire warmed my face and hands, stew bubbled in a cast-iron pot. I slept in a dark as thick as a wool blanket. In the morning a breeze stirred the ashes of my fire pit and a flame shot up.

God's words in God's pages made more sense to me in God's wild. After a few days I was a new man. God was as close to me as the sweet air I took into my lungs. In fact, he had never left my heart. Or left me without strength. It was just that I knew that better now. And lived again.

> As long as I live, I'll hear waterfalls and birds and winds sing. I'll interpret the rocks, learn the language of flood, storm, and the avalanche. I'll acquaint myself with the glaciers and wild gardens, and get as near the heart of the world as I can.[6]
>
> John Muir

> And I will make all my mountains a way, and my highways shall be exalted.
>
> Isaiah 49:11 KJV

> Let the mountains bring peace to the people, and the hills, in righteousness.
>
> Psalm 72:3 NASB

---

6. Linnie Marsh Wolfe, *Son of the Wilderness: The Life of John Muir* (Madison, WI: University of Wisconsin Press, 1945, 1973, 2003), 144.

Acknowledgments

Writing and editing a book for publication, especially a book like this that holds so much of my own heart and soul in it, is made immeasurably more incredible an experience by having a fine editor to work with. My thanks to Jon Wilcox for his blend of encouragement and challenge that helped make *Majestic and Wild* as free and strong as it could possibly be. My thanks also to the team from Baker who worked on the cover and all the marketing and promotion and who believed in what *M&W* was about and what it could mean to others. Always, my thanks to my beautiful wife, Linda, and my terrific children, Micah and Micaela, who shared so many of these stories with me in the stunning world of mountains and forests that seem to surround us wherever we go. My thanks to my friends for their support and prayers—they make such a difference—and to the animal companions who walked so many wilderness miles with me in all seasons and in all weather. And thank God. His big heart, his Son, and the wilderness he fashioned saved my life. I've lived a dream.

Murray Pura was born in Winnipeg, Manitoba, Canada, and has traveled extensively throughout Canada, the United States, Europe, Asia, and the Middle East. Ordained as a Baptist minister in 1986, Pura has served five churches in Canada and headlined numerous speaking engagements in Canada and the United States. He has fifteen books published; is a contributor to the *Life With God Bible;* and has been a finalist for The Paraclete Fiction Award, the Dartmouth Book Award, the John Spencer Hill Literary Award, and The Kobzar Literary Award of Toronto. He won the 2012 WORD Award (Toronto) for top historical fiction for the novel *The White Birds of Morning*, and his novel *The Wings of Morning* has been nominated for best inspirational romance of 2012 by the American Christian Fiction Writers (ACFW). Murray has an MDiv from Acadia University and Baptist Divinity School and a ThM and DCS from Regent College (Vancouver). He lives by the Rocky Mountains near Calgary, Alberta.